JACK

WHY I
BELIEVE

WHY I BELIEVE

Revised and Expanded

D. JAMES KENNEDY

WORD PUBLISHING

NASHVILLE

A Thomas Nelson Company

This book is affectionately
dedicated to my mother.

CONTENTS

ACKNOWLEDGMENTS

I would like to express my appreciation to Cay Hunter, who has proofread these messages and done the research for the documentation. Without her untiring efforts, this book would not be in print.

I would also like to express my appreciation to Ruth Rohm, who typed the original manuscripts and assisted in the documentation research.

INTRODUCTION

The Scripture states: "Be ready always to give an answer to every man that asketh you a reason of the hope that is in you with meekness and fear" (1 Peter 3:15). That is not simply good advice; it is a commandment from God!

Recently I happened to hear a call-in radio show that had as its guest an atheist who was expounding his views. While frantically trying to get a call through to the station, I listened to a dozen or more Christian callers talk to this man. I was appalled at the ease with which he was chewing them up and spitting them out. It seemed that every Christian who called was incapable of giving an intelligent reason for the faith that he or she held. "The Bible says such and such," each would begin in trying to support what she or he was saying. The atheist would counter: "Well, why do you believe the Bible?" Every one of them was reduced to stammering out something like, "Well, I've got it down in my heart." The atheist would answer, "Well, it's not down in my heart, friend, and I don't believe it."

I determined that it is especially important in these days for Christians to be able to give a reason for the hope that is in them and that I would try to do something practical to help. This book is the result. Challenges from unbelievers and non-Christian religions confront us all around. Television, books, magazines, and movies subject our faith to questioning in thousands of ways, large and small. As Christians who worship the One who is the incarnate *Logos*, or logic of God, we must be ready to speak to those who are openly antagonistic to our basic beliefs. We sin against God when we remain silent because we are incapable of defending them.

Not only that—when we do not stand ready with a reason for our hope and do not know why we believe what we believe, we give others the impression that Christianity is a religion based merely upon blind faith or emotional prejudice. Nothing could be further from the truth! We often accuse those who reject Christianity without at least examining the evidence for it of being prejudiced. Then is it not also true that if a person accepts Christianity without examining the evidence, that, too, is nothing other than prejudice or credulity?

The Bible tells us to examine all things and to hold fast to that which is good. Yet too frequently we are not willing to do that just because it takes a little intellectual effort on our part to become workmen who need not be ashamed. When we do not examine the grounds and foundation for our faith, we find that Satan will use our ignorance to attack our belief; and when we experience difficulties, he will sow doubts in our minds

It is my hope that in stating the reasons for my belief, I

may help Christian readers to clarify their own thinking and to become better able to articulate and defend their faith. I hope also that many who may not have come to a decision for Christ will be convinced by my arguments to take that step.

CHAPTER ONE

WHY I BELIEVE
IN THE BIBLE

I will raise them up a Prophet . . . and will put my words in his mouth; and he shall speak unto them all that I shall command him.

DEUTERONOMY 18:18

There are many reasons why I believe the Bible. The first one is the reason that God Himself gives: "I will raise them up a Prophet . . . and will put my words in his mouth" (Deuteronomy 18:18). Many people have claimed to be speaking for God, but are they indeed speaking for God or are they false prophets? God says that there is a way that you will be able to tell. "When a prophet speaketh in the name of the Lord, if the thing follow not, nor come to pass, that is the thing which the Lord hath not spoken, but the prophet hath spoken it presumptuously: thou shalt not be afraid of him" (18:22). "For I am God, and there is none else; I am God and there is none like me, declaring the end from the beginning, and from ancient times the things that are not

1

yet done" (Isaiah 46:9–10). "Hereby ye will know. . . ." It is a matter of predictive prophecy.

The Scripture says, "Despise not prophesyings. Prove all things; hold fast that which is good" (1 Thessalonians 5:20–21). Many people have despised the prophecies of God because they have never examined or proved them to determine if they are reliable and true. Perhaps this is because people suppose that prophecy is not real and genuine, or so commonplace that it can be easily explained. The biblical prophecies are quite specific, real, and genuine; they are unique because they do not exist anywhere else.

In all the writings of Buddha, Confucius, and Lao-tse, you will not find a single example of predicted prophecy. In the Koran (the writings of Muhammad) there is one instance of a specific prophecy—a self-fulfilling prophecy—that he, Muhammad himself, would return to Mecca. Quite different from the prophecy of Jesus who said that He would return from the grave. One is easily fulfilled, and the other is impossible to any human being.

Jeanne Dixon has probably had the most name recognition of any so-called prophet in America. Can she foretell the future? She's made some clever guesses, but do they accurately come to pass as do the prophecies of the Scripture? During the three presidential elections held in 1952, 1956, and 1960, Jeane Dixon prophesied who the candidate would be for each of the major parties in all three of those elections, as well as who would win each election. How did she do? She missed all of the candidates, all of the parties, and all of the winners of all the elections.

My wife saved an article from the *National Enquirer*

magazine many years ago, which contained the predictions of the ten leading seers or prophets in the world today for the events that were supposed to take place the last six months of that year.[1] I examined all of those sixty-one prophecies carefully. Do you know how many of them were actually fulfilled? Not one! It seemed to me that if a person predicted sixty-one things, he or she ought to be lucky enough to hit at least one. Perhaps God wanted to show people how incapable they are of predicting the future.

A great historian, Dr. John H. Gerstner, has said that historians know how difficult it is to predict the future because the wheels of the future turn on so many "ifs." What about the Scripture? In the Old Testament alone there are two thousand predictive prophecies—not a few lucky guesses. Someone will say, "Well, they are just sort of vague generalities, like the sayings of the Delphic Oracle or the Sibylline Oracles. Maxentius, emperor of Rome, is said to have come to one of the Sibylline Oracles and asked what would happen if he attacked the army of Constantine that was approaching Rome on the other side of the Tiber River. The Oracle's answer was: "In that day, the enemy of Rome will be destroyed." So, confident of victory, he attacked Constantine's army, but it was Maxentius who was destroyed. The Oracle failed to define who the enemy of Rome really was; thus in the pattern of most oracular utterances, however it turned out, the prophecy was fulfilled.

The prophecies of the Scripture, on the other hand, are incredibly specific and detailed. They must be exactly fulfilled. The prophecies cannot possibly be just good guesses because they concerned themselves with things that had no likelihood of ever coming to pass. They predicted the very opposite of the natural expectations of human beings. They cannot have been written after the events and pawned off as prophecies because in hundreds of instances the fulfillment of the prophecy did not take place until hundreds of years after the death of the prophet. In many cases, the fulfillment came after the completion of the Old Testament and even its translation into Greek in 150 B.C.

What are some of these incredibly specific and amazing prophecies? Some two thousand specific prophecies have already been fulfilled. For example, they deal with scores of cities with which Israel had dealings and with dozens of nations contiguous with or near Israel. The entire futurity of those nations and cities is described in the Old Testament, and its accuracy can be verified by anyone who has a good encyclopedia.

Consider the prophecies concerning Tyre and Sidon, two great cities of the eastern coast of the Mediterranean. Tyre was to the sea what Babylon was to the land. The great city of Carthage was simply one of the daughters of Tyre, and yet at its height, the prophet in the Old Testament declared that the city of Tyre would be destroyed, never to be rebuilt, and never again to be inhabited (Ezekiel 26:19–21). He warned the city of Sidon that the inhabitants would be decimated, but the city would continue (28:21–23). The facts are that the city of Sidon was attacked, it was betrayed by its own king, forty thousand of the inhabitants were killed; but the city of Sidon continues until this time.

What happened to the city of Tyre? These are some of the specific prophecies about it. Ezekiel declared when Tyre was at its height: "And they shall destroy the walls of Tyrus, and break down her towers: I will also scrape her dust from her, and make her like the top of a rock. It shall be a place for the spreading of nets in the midst of the sea: for I have spoken it, saith the Lord God. . . . And they shall lay thy stones and thy timber and thy dust in the midst of the water. . . . And I will make thee like the top of a rock . . . thou shalt be built no more: for I the Lord have spoken it" (Ezekiel 26:4–5, 12–14). A few years after the writing of this prophecy, the great Nebuchadnezzar of Babylon brought his army to Tyre and laid siege to the city. For thirteen years the city of Tyre withstood the efforts of the king of Babylon. Finally the walls of the city crumbled, and the hordes of the Babylonian army poured into the city and put its remaining inhabitants to the sword. Thousands, however, had fled into the sea by boat to form the new city of Tyre on an island a half mile out in the Mediterranean. The prophecy was fulfilled, therefore, only in part.

Some might say that Ezekiel wrote this prophecy after the events happened, but that is impossible. Centuries went by. Two hundred fifty years later, when Ezekiel had long been moldering in his grave, most of the walls of Tyre still stood jutting into the sky—mute testimony to the fact that the prophecy had not been fulfilled. Millions of tons of stone, rubble, and timbers were left, and yet God had said the city would be scraped clean like the top of a rock—that the stones and the timbers and the very dust of the city would be cast into the sea. What madman could possibly come along two hundred fifty years later and complete this unfulfilled prophecy? It seemed as if God was wrong; yet the Bible had declared, "I the Lord have spoken it."

Then, like a bugle call, there came a thrill of terror out of the north, as a mighty conqueror appeared on the horizon. Alexander the Great was poised at the Strait of the Dardanelles readying his attack on the dominant Persian Empire. He crossed that strait and gave to the king of Persia his first crushing defeat. The mighty Persian army turned and fled to the south, then inland to the east, with Alexander in hot pursuit. However, before turning inland to follow the fleeing army, Alexander, as a great strategist, decided to nullify the effects of the mighty Persian navy. He sealed off all the ports on the eastern end of the Mediterranean. One after another, the cities capitulated and surrendered. Finally Alexander came to new Tyre, built with impregnable walls a half mile out in the Mediterranean. He commanded the city to surrender. When its inhabitants laughed at his command, Alexander, with his chief engineer, Diades, conceived the boldest and most daring plan in the history of warfare: They would build a causeway across the half mile of the Mediterranean Sea to the island of new Tyre. Where would they find the materials for such a causeway? The order was issued by the great king: "Tear down the walls of Tyre, take the timbers and the stones, the rubble and the logs, and cast them into the sea." So the great army of Alexander obediently began to fulfill the word of God.

A few years ago, I purchased a little book on Alexander the Great by Charles Mercer, with consultant Cornelius C. Vermeule III, the curator of classical art at the Museum of Fine Arts in Boston. This book contains a most amazing description of these events: "Mainland Tyre was leveled, and its rubble was carried to the construction site. Meanwhile, logs were dragged from the forests of Lebanon, and quarries were opened in the hills to supply stones for Diades's fabulous highway. . . . Alexander himself carried stones on his back."[2] "Rubble, logs, stones!" These are the very same objects that the prophet Ezekiel talked about thousands of years ago. The stones and the timbers and the dust were carried and cast into the sea. History tells us that they scraped the very city itself to get everything they could to make this highway in order to destroy the new city of Tyre. New Tyre was finally besieged, destroyed, and leveled.

But the prophecy still was not completely fulfilled. God had said that He would destroy the walls of Tyrus and make her like the top of a rock. He said that it would become a place for the spreading of nets. A member of my church recently visited the city of Tyre and returned with pictures of new Tyre. They showed nets spread out on the flat rock that once had been the proud city of Tyre. "For I have spoken it, saith the Lord God" (Ezekiel 26:5). Let any unbeliever explain those prophecies!

Consider two other cities—Samaria and Jerusalem. Samaria was the capital of the Northern Kingdom of Israel; Jerusalem was the capital of the Southern Kingdom of Judah. While those cities were both in their prime, the prophets declared that not only would Jerusalem be destroyed and its inhabitants carried away, but the wall would also be destroyed (Jeremiah 24:9; 29:21; 35:17). The prophets further said that the city and the wall would be rebuilt, and the people would be brought back (Isaiah 4:3–6). Concerning Samaria, the prophets said that its walls would be cast down; that it would be made into a vineyard; that the foundations thereof would be uncovered (Micah 1:5–6). What about the walls of Jerusalem? They were destroyed, but they have been rebuilt. I have walked along the top of the great walls of Jerusalem.

Concerning my visit to Samaria, I remember three things about that city. Later, I learned that these are the three specific prophecies that are mentioned in Scripture. I recall looking down from a steep wall on a high mountain and seeing in the valley huge stones that had once been the walls of Samaria. I also remember our guide pointing out the vineyards, the olive trees, and various other trees. I recall seeing the great excavations in the ground going down thirty or forty feet, showing the foundations of the great fortresses that once had been Samaria. "I will make Samaria as an heap of the field, and as plantings of a vineyard: and I will pour down the stones thereof into the valley, and I will discover the foundations thereof" (Micah 1:6). What if the wall of Jerusalem were destroyed today? What if the walls of Samaria were rebuilt? The prophecy would be shown to be false.

What were the prophecies concerning the cities of Edom? Edom was a nation near the Dead Sea that withstood the people of God, so God pronounced a curse upon Edom. He said: "I am against thee, and I will stretch out mine hand against thee, and I will make thee most desolate. I will lay thy cities waste, and thou shalt be desolate, and thou shalt know that I am the Lord. . . . I will make thee perpetual desolations, and thy cities shall not return: and ye shall know that I am the Lord" (Ezekiel 35:3–4, 9). Alexander Keith has collected statements by skeptics concerning these prophecies. (The skeptics had no idea that they were making any reference to prophecies but merely to these places.) Constantine Volney, the skeptic who was responsible for Lincoln's skepticism, said concerning Edom that "the traces of many towns are met with. At present all this country is a desert." The noted Swiss explorer and traveler John L. Burkhardt declares that the whole plain presented to the view an expanse of shifting sands. Stephen, a Christian standing among the ruins of Petra, one of the great cities of Edom, declares, "Would that the skeptic could stand as I did among the ruins of this city, among the rocks, and there open the Sacred Book, and read the words of the inspired penman, written when this desolate place was one of the greatest cities of the world. I could see the scoff arrested, his cheek pale, his lips quivering, and his heart quaking with fear, as the ruined city cries out to him in a voice loud and powerful as that of one risen from the dead. Though he would not believe Moses and the prophets, he believes the handwriting of God Himself and the desolation and eternal ruin around him."

Consider the magnificent city of Babylon, perhaps the greatest city in ancient times. The walls were fourteen or fifteen miles long. The city consisted of one hundred ninety-six square miles of the most beautiful architecture, hanging gardens and palaces, temples and towers. She drew her stores from no foreign country. She invented an alphabet, worked out the problems of arithmetic, invented implements for measuring time, and advanced beyond all previous peoples in science. Yet God said of Babylon when it was the greatest city in the world: "Babylon, the glory of kingdoms, the beauty of the Chaldees' excellency, shall be as when God overthrew Sodom and Gomorrah" (Isaiah 13:19).

There are more than one hundred specific prophecies concerning Babylon's fate. Consider the great walls of Babylon. The historian Herodotus tells us that these walls had towers that extended above the 200-foot walls to a height of 300 feet. The walls were 187 feet thick at the base and enclosed an area of 196 square miles. The city of Babylon was impregnable. But God said of those towers and that city: "The broad walls of Babylon shall be utterly broken. . . . It shall be desolate for ever" (Jeremiah 51:58, 62). Is that prophecy vague or ambiguous? In no way!

The Great Wall of China is not nearly as large or as strong; though it is older, it still stands today. The walls of Jerusalem still stand. But what about the walls of Babylon? Major Keppel says, in the *Narrative* of his travels, "We totally failed to discover any trace of the city walls." The walls of Babylon were destroyed, but only gradually. The prophet could not possibly have written his prediction after the event because the fulfillment of the prophecy was not completed until after the time of Christ. The Old Testament had been completed and translated into Greek five hundred years before.

In the fourth century A.D., Julian the Apostate came to the throne of Rome. His one overwhelming desire was to destroy Christianity and reestablish the pagan religions of Rome. While engaged in a war with the Persians near the remains of Babylon, Julian completely destroyed the remnants of the wall of Babylon, lest it afford any protection in the future for the Persian army. Thus the prophecy was brought to fulfillment by one of Scripture's greatest antagonists of all time.

But God had much more to say about this city: "Because

of the wrath of the Lord it shall not be inhabited, but it shall be wholly desolate. . . . It shall be no more inhabited for ever" (Jeremiah 50:13, 39). Could anything be more specific than that? Have these prophecies been fulfilled? I have seen pictures of Babylon. It is a trackless waste of huge mounds and heaps, inhabited only by the jackal, the viper, and the scorpion. Skeptics themselves have described it as nothing but heaps; they tell us that ruins compose the only remains of Babylon. Ruins like those of Babylon, composed of heaps of rubbish impregnated with niter, cannot be cultivated. Babylon, whose fields around the city were so fertile that Herodotus refused to write about them lest people think him insane, now can grow nothing because God has doomed the area to perpetual desolation, and not a blade of grass will survive. It is a barren desert. The ruins were nearly the only indication that it had ever been inhabited.

Consider these two specific but apparently contradictory prophecies. "The sea is come up upon Babylon: she is covered with the multitude of the waves thereof" (Jeremiah 51:42). The other prophecy describes Babylon as, "a desolation, a dry land, and a wilderness" (v. 43). Now note that amazing fulfillment. Claudius James Rich, in his *Narrative of a Journey to the Site of Babylon in 1811*, points out: "For the space of two months throughout the year the ruins of Babylon are inundated by the annual overflowing of the Euphrates so as to render many parts of them inaccessible by converting the valleys into morasses." After the subsiding of the waters, even the low heaps again become sunburned ruins, and the site of Babylon, like that of other cities of Chaldea, is a dry waste, a parched and burning plain. But God said it would never be

built again—a prophecy totally contrary to all the expectations of the past, where every city of the Near East that had
been destroyed had been built again. Babylon was situated in
the most fertile part of the Euphrates valley, and yet twenty-
five hundred years have come and gone, and Babylon to this
day remains an uninhabited waste.

God said the city would not be built again, yet the mightiest man the world had ever seen—Alexander the Great—
decided that he would rebuild Babylon. Coming across the
ruins of Babylon, he determined to make this the capital of
his worldwide empire. He issued six hundred thousand
rations to his soldiers to rebuild the city of Babylon. Would
God be disproved? History records the fact that immediately
after making the declaration to rebuild Babylon, Alexander
the Great was struck dead, and the whole enterprise was
abandoned. For God had said it would never be built again.

These are a dozen or so of the two thousand such specific
prophecies in the Old Testament alone. I believe that those
who say that the Bible was written by men are simply
expressing their own ignorance of the subject. There is nothing like it in all the literature of the world, religious or irre-
ligious. The hand that wrote these Scriptures was the hand
of none other than that One who could say, "I am the first
and the last; I am the beginning and the end, I am he that
knows all things. I am he that declares the things that are not
yet come to pass." Predictions are also promises. I believe
that God gave us more than two thousand predictions in
order that we may learn to believe His promises. God
promised that the walls of Jerusalem would be rebuilt; that
the walls of Babylon would never be rebuilt; that Tyre would

be destroyed; that Sidon would continue—so that we may believe His promises.

He also promised that he that believeth on the Son shall never die, but have everlasting life; and he that believeth not the Son shall not see life, but shall have the wrath of God upon him forever. The truthfulness of those words and the certainty of their fulfillment are attested to by more than two thousand prophecies that have already come to pass. Those who disregard them have no one to blame for their own destruction but themselves.

Stuart Atkinson
Erwin Berry
: would enjoy reading
This chapter also

CHAPTER TWO

THE STONES
CRY OUT . . .

*And he answered and said unto them, I tell you that,
if these should hold their peace, the stones would
immediately cry out.*

LUKE 19:40

During the last part of the eighteenth century, what was known as the higher critical school began to develop in Germany and reached its zenith in the middle of the nineteenth century. Literary scholars of this era based all of their conclusions on literary presuppositions. They tore the Bible apart and then put it together again, completely differently. Jesus Christ had said that if His followers would hold their peace concerning His praise, the very stones would cry out. When leading Christian scholars began to hold their peace by thus attacking the Bible, God began to fulfill that prediction, and the stones began to cry out.

Along with the growth of the higher critical school came

the growth of archaeology, a science begun in the early nineteenth century. Many people wondered whether archaeology would confirm the findings of higher criticism or confirm a belief in the historicity of the Bible. Would fancy be substantiated by fact or would the fancies of the critics give way to the facts?

Perhaps you have wondered why the Bible is filled with so many details that seem to be excrescencies to the major message of the Word. The thirty-third chapter of Numbers, for instance, contains a list of forty-two different sites that were used in the Exodus. In other places, scores of cities, places, kings, and individuals are mentioned. Readers often get bogged down in the "begats," the people, and the history and wonder why we couldn't take all of that out and get down to the message. The fact is that in trying to edit the Scripture, one discovers oneself cutting out vital organs unknowingly. The scholar R. A. Torrey said that "the plethora of details were watermarks in paper, which bear indelible evidence of the time and plan of manufacture."[1] As a detective can ascertain from a watermark many things about the paper—its source, for instance—the science of archaeology has uncovered from these details a vast wealth of information about the Scripture.

In a courtroom, lawyers frequently ask witnesses many detailed questions that do not seem to bear directly on the issue at hand. They are attempting to establish in all sorts of corroborative ways whether the witness is telling the truth or is lying. According to one historian, it is impossible to establish a lie in the midst of a well-known history. As the details are brought out and confirmed or denied, so the truth of the story also is confirmed or denied. One scholar states: "To my mind, absolute truth and local details (a thing which cannot possibly be invented when it is spread over a history covering many centuries) give proof almost absolute as to the truth of the thing related. Such proof we have for every part of the Bible."

The distinguished German scholar and orientalist Julius Wellhausen had overwhelming academic credentials that caused people to listen to what he said. In 1889 he still subjected the fourteenth chapter of Genesis to critical attack. This chapter relates that four kings from Mesopotamia and Babylonia came over into Palestine and attacked a group of five kings around the Dead Sea, including the kings of Sodom and Gomorrah. They conquered these kings and carried off goods and many captives, among whom was a young man by the name of Lot, Abram's nephew. On learning of this, Abram gathered his servants and took off in pursuit, overtaking the invaders near Damascus (quite a journey north) and engaging them in battle. Having discomfited his enemy, Abram rescued Lot, his family, and all his goods.

The critics insisted, first of all, that there was no intercourse between Babylonia and Palestine. In those days, they said, travel of that sort was unheard of and could not possibly have happened. Wellhausen stated: "That four kings from the Persian Gulf should, 'in the time of Abraham,' have made an incursion into the Sinaitic peninsula, that they should on this occasion have attacked five kinglets on the Dead Sea Littoral and have carried them off prisoners, and finally that Abraham should have set out in pursuit of the retreating victors accompanied by 318 men servants, and have forced them to disgorge their prey—all these incidents are sheer impossibilities which gain nothing in credibility from the fact that they are placed in a world which had passed away."[2]

Now that world has come to light again. From its tombs and varied places, voices cry out from the dead, and that world of impossibility has changed considerably. Wellhausen was not the only one who had such an opinion. That great critic Theodor Noldeke said criticism had forever disproved the Bible's claim to be historical.[3] Yet that is exactly the claim of the fourteenth chapter of Genesis.

As a result of extensive excavations in 1890 in the dry sands of Egypt by Dr. Flinders Petrie and others, we now know who these four kings from the Persian Gulf were. Transliterating from the Semitic to the Babylonian, we discover that the king who is called Amraphel is none other than the very famous man whom we know in secular history as Hammurabi. The great Hammurabi, who gave us his code of laws, and three other kings descended upon and attacked these kings at the Dead Sea. All of this has now been demonstrated to be historical fact beyond question. Their names have been ascertained, as have the sites where they camped.[4]

Another source of delight for the critics was that the Bible mentions hundreds of kings, peoples, cities, and even whole nations that were not mentioned by the historians of antiquities nor in all of secular literature. If the historians never mentioned a nation, obviously that nation did not exist. One of the "mythical" nations that the Jews supposedly fought with was the Hittites, who are mentioned in eight different chapters in the Old Testament. One leading archaeologist said he did not believe there ever were such people as the Hittites.

When Dr. Hugo Winckler went to the area to dig where the Hittites were supposed to have lived, he discovered more than forty of their cities, including their capital, along with a great number of monuments describing their activities.[5] Commenting on a treaty between the Hittites and the Egyptians that the Bible describes, one English critic said there was no more chance for a treaty to have existed between the Egyptians and the Hittites than between England and the Choctaws. Yet spelled out on a palace wall in one of the uncovered cities of Egypt was found the whole treaty between Egypt and the Hittites! Numerous Babylonian inscriptions have now proved the Hittites to have been a great superpower located between Egypt and Babylonia, so large that all of Egypt and Babylonia were considered to have been tribes of the Hittites.

The Bible tells us that the pharaoh oppressed the Israelites and caused them to build for him the store cities of Pithom and Raamses. We remember the story of how they first built with mortar and straw. Then they had to gather their own straw, and finally they had to build the bricks without any straw at all (Exodus 5). When Sir Flinders Petrie later discovered the sites of Pithom and Raamses, he noted some incredible things about them. They were built with mortar—something found nowhere else in Egypt. Moreover, the lower layers were built of brick that used stubble instead of straw. In the second and upper layers were bricks made without straw.

For over a hundred years the critics have said that Moses did not write the Pentateuch at all. But Dr. William F. Albright of Johns Hopkins University, probably the most outstanding American archaeologist of the twentieth century, says, "It is, accordingly, sheer hypercriticism to deny the substantially Mosaic character of the Pentateuchal tradition."[6]

Then there was the story about Jericho. Joshua fought the Battle of Jericho, but the critics said that it never happened. One does not just walk around a city and have the walls fall down flat. But what did Professor John Garstang, British archaeologist and authority on Hittite civilization, discover when he came to the site of Jericho to dig? He stated: "As for the main fact, there remains no doubt the walls fell outward so completely that the attackers would be able to clamber up and over their ruins into the city."[7] Why is that so unusual? Because walls do not fall outward. Ordinarily they fall inward, but in this case the walls were made by some superior power to fall outward, as the Bible says. The critics also declared that the account is obviously fatuous because it says that the Israelites marched around the city seven times in one day. You could not walk around a modern city of one hundred thousand people seven times in one day, and Jericho was described as a great city. But Garstang's investigation provided an interesting fact about Jericho—it was smaller than the sites upon which many large metropolitan churches are built. Having been to Jericho many times, I know that I could walk around it seven times in one morning and play a set of tennis before lunch! Again the critics were proved wrong.

Albright states: "Until recently it was the fashion among biblical historians to treat the patriarchal sagas of Genesis as though they were artificial creations of Israelite scribes of the time of the divided monarchy. Or perhaps they were tales told by imaginative rhapsodists around Israelite campfires."[8] "Archaeological discoveries since 1925 have changed all of this. Aside from a few diehards among older scholars, there is scarcely a single biblical historian who has not been impressed by the rapid accumulation of data supporting the substantial historicity of the patriarchal tradition."[9]

An article by one of these diehards that recently appeared in the *Miami Herald* declaimed that there was not one biblical scholar who would maintain that the Gospels of Matthew, Mark, Luke, and John were written by the authors whose names they bear. He said that every scholar knows this, and nobody believes that they wrote those books. Apparently this man had read one book by someone who had come to this conclusion, a conclusion fashionable in the nineteenth century when it was supposed that those Gospels were written in the second and third centuries. Now manuscripts have been found that are dated one hundred years earlier than that. Yet diehards still spout off nineteenth-century critical conclusions that have been so discredited in recent times. "Many an archaeologist has been impressed by what he has found," said Albright. A number of archaeologists have not only been impressed; they have also been converted.

One of the most notable of these was Sir William Ramsay. He was an atheist, the son of atheists; he was wealthy and a Ph.D. from Oxford. He gave his whole life over to archaeology and determined that he would disprove the Bible. He set out for the Holy Land and decided to disprove the Book of Acts. After twenty-five or more years (he had released book after book during this time), he was incredibly impressed by the accuracy of Luke in his writings and finally declared that Luke was exact, down to the most minute details. In his attempts to disprove the Bible, Sir William Ramsay uncovered hundreds of things that confirmed the historicity of the Book of Acts. Finally, in one of his books he shocked the whole critical world by declaring himself to be a Christian.[10] The world's greatest authority on the Book of Acts and the travels of the apostle Paul was converted by his digging, as have been numerous other archaeologists over the centuries.

Daniel was another book that especially delighted those who were trying to discredit the Bible. One of the many things they attempted to disprove in that book was the idea that Belshazzar was the last king of Babylon and that he died on the day Cyrus and his army entered the city of Babylon. Secular historians had declared that though the Bible says Belshazzar was the son of Nebuchadnezzar, Nabonidus was the son of Nebuchadnezzar, and Nabonidus was the last king of Babylon.

Dean Farrar, one of the critics, said, "Belshazzar—history knows of no such king."[11] If a secular historian says one thing and the Bible says the other, obviously the Bible must be incorrect. This presupposition is so pervasive in the minds of the critics that it is amazing how they make such conclusions continually, regardless of what the facts reveal.

In the city of Ur of the Chaldeans of Babylon, four clay cylinders of King Nabonidus were discovered. They dealt with the building of the Temple of the Moon God, which contained a prayer to that god for the king's son, Belshazzar. It was discovered that Belshazzar and Nabonidus jointly ruled Babylon. While Nabonidus was out in the country, Belshazzar ruled in the capital. Further, one of these cylinders stated that Gobryas (the general of Cyrus's army) entered Babylon, and Belshazzar died that day. Belshazzar is mentioned numerous times regarding contracts that he entered into, farmlands that he bought, and other such things.[12] Again the critical bubble burst!

The archaeological confirmation of the Flood of Noah's time is enormous. Stories of the Nochian Flood have been found in almost every civilization in the world. Among the most interesting are those found in Babylonia and Acadia. They provide substantially the same description except for the perversions that had entered into the later Babylonian version, written about eight hundred years after the Mosaic account.

In Babylon also is a tablet on which one of the Babylonian kings mentions his enjoyment in reading the writings of those who lived before the Flood. Arguments that writing did not even exist in the time of Moses have now been answered with the knowledge that five hundred years before Moses, in the time of Abraham, there were libraries with thousands of volumes. We know that well over a thousand years before the time of Abraham, in fact, writing was practiced, and now we have records of those who wrote even before the Flood.

Another Babylonian tablet gives an interesting confirmation. Noah was the tenth generation from Adam according to the Bible, and this Babylonian tablet names the ten kings of Babylon who lived before the Flood. Another tablet names all the kings of Babylon, and after the first ten there are the words: "The Deluge came up. . . ." Then the tablets continue.

The spades of the archaeologists have uncovered innumerable facts that confirm the Scripture. More than twenty-five thousand sites have been discovered that pertain to the Bible. Records of tens of thousands of individuals and events also have been found. The most recent and continuing testimony of archaeology, like all such testimony that has gone before, is definitely and uniformly favorable to the Scripture at its face value, rather than to the Scripture as reconstructed by critics. Dr. William Albright says: "There can be no doubt that archaeology has confirmed the substantial historicity of the Old Testament tradition."[13]

The excessive skepticism shown toward the Bible by the important historical-critical schools of the eighteenth and nineteenth centuries, which placed all sorts of phases of the Bible later than they were before, has been discredited by discovery after discovery. The accuracy of innumerable details has brought increased recognition of the value of the Bible as a source of history. Millar Burrows of Yale observes: "In many cases archaeology has refuted the views of modern critics. In a number of instances it has been shown that these views rest on false assumptions and unreal artificial schemes of historical development. The excessive skepticism of many liberal theologians stems not from careful evaluation of the available data, but from an enormous predisposition against the supernatural."

Sir Frederic Kenyon of the British Museum, one of the great scholars of our time, also points to the fact that archaeology has confirmed the Scripture. Nelson Glueck, the renowned Jewish archaeologist, said, "It may be stated categorically that no archaeological discovery has ever controverted a biblical reference." He continued his assertion of "the almost incredibly accurate historical memory of the Bible, particularly when we see that it is fortified by historical fact." He categorically declared that no archaeological finding has controverted a biblical fact reference.[14]

We see again that as the critics were ceasing to praise Christ, just as God said, the stones have begun to cry out! Through all the recent researches in Palestine, Assyria, Babylonia, Egypt, and other places, those stones have shown that the Scripture is indeed the inspired Word of God. In tens of thousands of details the Scripture has been shown to be true.

It is not because of any want of historical data that people do not believe the Scripture or do not believe in Christ. Rather, it is because of a want of a moral disposition to surrender one's life to the Lordship and authority of Jesus Christ. It is the moral problem that confronts most unbelievers.

These again are some more of the reasons why I believe in the Bible. I believe in the Christ whom it portrays and whom it presents to us as the living, risen, glorified Savior who can bring forgiveness, peace, joy, and assurance to all those who will repent of their sins and place their trust in Him who died for us. "If these should hold their peace, the stones would cry out."

CHAPTER THREE

WHY I BELIEVE
IN GOD

The fool hath said in his heart, There is no God.
Corrupt are they, and have done abominable iniquity:
there is none that doeth good.

PSALM 53:1

Is there a God or not? This question eclipses all other questions that mankind might ask. Should you feel that statement is the opinion of a theologian or a preacher, then listen to this statement found in *The Great Ideas Syntopicon*, the crucial study guide for the Great Books series, a remarkable collection of most of the combined wisdom of Western civilization from the time of Thales to the present. Mortimer Adler states, "With the exception of certain mathematicians and physicists, all authors of the Great Books are represented in the chapter on God."[1] The reason is obvious. More consequences for thought and action follow the affirmation or denial of God than the answering of any other basic question. The whole tenor of human life is affected by whether men regard themselves as the supreme being in the universe, or acknowledge a superhuman being whom they conceive of as an object of fear or love and a force to be defied or a Lord to be obeyed. The significance of this question and the evidence for the existence of God are the great debate for and against atheism. For most of this century, militant atheism has spread like a deadly fungus across our world to the point that the twentieth century has been called the century of atheism. But the times are a-changing. As the twentieth century has been called the century of atheism, the twenty-first century, as an increasing number of intellectuals are saying, is probably going to be a century of spirituality. The pillars of secularism, atheism, and materialism are crumbling.

Many modern sophisticated Americans have, for decades, believed that somehow science has disproved God or, as Julian Huxley said, they have reduced Him "to simply the disappearing smile of the Cheshire cat."

Yet in his book *God, the Atom, and the Universe*, James Reid states: "Science is preparing a surprise for mankind. At least it will be a surprise for those who have doubts about the Bible and its God. It will also come as a surprise for those who are laboring under the misapprehension that science has undermined the Bible. In fact, it may even shock some scientists, who may be startled to find that their newly uncovered fact, or accepted theory, provides still another link in the chain of evidence that is showing that the facts of the universe support the Bible's statements—including creation."[2] He further states that for years, as a man of science, he had endeavored under the old classic physics, the Newtonian physics, to discover support for these in the Bible, but the new disciplines of quantum physics—quantum theory and quantum mechanics—have totally transformed the scientific world. Now he *is* discovering that true science supports the statements of the Scripture.

As the old classical physics gave way to the new quantum physics, a whole new concept of the universe emerged. As Einstein's theory of relativity revealed the inner relationship of mass and energy, he suddenly found that the new discoveries of science were establishing the teachings of the Scripture. The facts of the universe are supported increasingly by the findings of science, and the consequences of this are incalculable.[3]

The result of the years and years of creeping atheism taught by this century's scientists, however, has taken its toll. We live in a time of relativistic morality that does not believe in a God to whom men are responsible. I believe this thought is basically responsible for the enormous incidence of crime, murder, rape, robbery, and every conceivable civil evil that we face in our society today. I have heard scores of men, supposedly knowledgeable on the subject, discuss a variety of remedies for the situation, and I am amazed at their incredible blindness. It seems that none of them realize it is the rampant denial of the God of the Bible that has caused men to become increasingly animalistic. Teach men that they are animals, and eventually they will act like animals.

E. L. Woodward, Oxford's professor of modern history, states: "The values of our Western heritage, justice, mercy, kindness, tolerance, self-sacrifice, are incompatible with materialism . . ."[4]—materialism being the view of the universe that there exists nothing but matter—no soul, no spirit—no God. "If I may borrow a well-worn phrase about the State [which he borrows from Marx] these values will wither away in a materialist culture." He further states that "it is meaningless to talk about human 'rights' in a materialistic society; one might as well make a moral appeal to the Atlantic Ocean."

There is no branch of science that looks at a larger portion of God's handiwork than do astronomers. The Scripture says: "The heavens declare the glory of God; and the firmament showeth his handiwork" (Psalm 19:1); "For the invisible things of him from the creation of the world are clearly seen" (Romans 1:20). Ninety percent of all astronomers today believe in God! Those who have most thoroughly examined His handiwork believe in God. That is a higher percentage than will be found of butchers, bakers, or candlestick-makers. Those who have looked most intently and to the farthest extent that man has been able to see in the universe have concluded that the hand that made it is Divine.

Dr. Robert Jastrow, one of the world's great astronomers, is founder and director of the Goddard Institute for Space Studies at NASA. In his blockbuster book, *God and the Astronomers*, he says "strange developments" are going on in astronomy. One of these was the discovery that the universe had a beginning. And that means that there had to be a "Beginner." As Jastrow put it, "The scientist has scaled the mountains of ignorance; he is about to conquer the highest peak, and as he pulls himself over the final rock, he is greeted by a band of theologians who have been sitting there for centuries."

Pierre Simon de La Place, one of the greatest of our astronomers, said that the proof in favor of an intelligent God as the author of creation stood as infinity to unity against any other hypothesis of ultimate causation; that it was infinitely more probable that a set of writing implements thrown promiscuously against parchment would produce Homer's *Iliad,* than that creation was originated by any cause other than God. The evidence for God as opposed to the evidence against Him as the Creator of this universe was as infinity to one. It could not even be measured.[5]

The most monumental book on science written in the nineties, in my opinion, was written by sixty notable scientists including twenty-four Nobel prize winners. The title of the book is *Cosmos, Bios & Theos*—in English that means "Universe, Life, and God." The coeditor of that book, Yale physicist and Nobel Laureate Professor Henry Margenau, concludes that "there is only one convincing answer" for the intricate laws that exist in nature. What does this Nobel Laureate physicist professor believe is the only convincing answer to the intricate laws that have been discovered in the universe? Evolution? No. What he believes is the answer is "creation by an omnipotent-omniscient God."

There are many different arguments for the existence of God. One is known as the cosmological argument. Though Kant and Hume directed their attacks at the various classical arguments for God, they did so without suitable evidence and without sufficient proof to refute them. Since the various theistic proofs are not mathematical (they are really arguments for overwhelming probability), these arguments still stand, and the mind of the creature still recognizes in them evidence of a Divine Creator. Sir James Jeans, one of the greatest of modern astronomers, said that the more he examined the vast expanses of space and the tremendous complexity of these things, the more the universe seemed to be one gigantic thought of a great mathematician.

The cosmological argument comes from the term *cosmos,* which means "the universe" and from which we get the word *cosmetic.* It means "ordered and beautiful," and there is within the universe so much evidence of order that it would be impossible to list it all. Quantum physics has demonstrated that at the level of subatomic particles, there is an irresistible urge of electrons toward symmetry and that there is an amazing cosmetic aspect to the universe. One author said that nature is a great architect, meaning that nature is God. It is also a great astronomer, a great chemist, a great physiologist, a great psychologist, and a great mathematician, demonstrating an incredible knowledge of the facts of the various sciences now known to mankind, which have all said the same thing.

There is also the teleological argument. The word *telos* in Greek means "the end," and teleology is that view of philosophy that sees that in the universe things are designed for a purpose, for an end. Atheists and evolutionists (they must almost invariably be one and the same) detest the word *purpose* or *teleology* because they believe that the world has no purpose. They believe it is all one gigantic accident, simply the concatenation of atoms that happened to come together in a chance fashion. Although people may say that things exist in an incredibly complex way and that is the only reason why we are here, it is hard for the human mind to disregard the fantastic number of evidences that Someone has been providing for our well-being.

Consider the mass and size of this planet upon which we have been placed. It is just right. Dr. Wallace says that if the earth were either 10 percent larger or 10 percent smaller than it is, life would not be possible upon this planet. Furthermore, it is just the right distance from the sun, and thus we receive the right amount of heat and light. If it were farther away, we would freeze, and if it were closer (such as the distance of Mercury or Venus) we would not be able to survive.[6]

Consider the amazing fact of the tilt of the axis of the earth. None of the other planets is tilted as ours is—23 degrees. This angle provides that the earth is slowly turned in all parts of its surface before the rays of the sun, much as a chicken would be turned upon a spit. If there were no tilt to the axis, the poles would accumulate enormous masses of ice, and the center part of the earth would become intensely hot.

Another amazing aspect of our relationship in the solar system is our moon. Many people do not realize that without the moon it would be impossible to live on this planet. If anyone were ever to succeed in deflecting the moon from its orbit, all life would cease on this planet. God has provided the moon as a maid to clean up the oceans and the shores of all our continents. Without the tides created by the moon, all our harbors and shores would become one stench pool of garbage, and it would be impossible to live anywhere near them. Because of the tides, continuous waves break upon the shores of the ocean, aerating the oceans of this planet and providing oxygen for the plankton, which is the very foundation of the food chain of our world. Without the plankton, there would not be oxygen, and man would not be able to live upon this earth. God has made the moon the right size and placed it the right distance from the earth to perform these and numerous other functions.

There is the wonder of our atmosphere. We live under a great ocean of air—78 percent nitrogen, 21 percent oxygen, and the other 1 percent is made up of almost a dozen different trace elements. Spectrographic studies of other planets in the stellar universe show that no other atmosphere, no other part of the known universe is made up of these same ingredients or anything like this composition. These elements are not chemically combined but are continually mixed mechanically by the tidal effect of the moon upon the atmosphere. This has the same effect that it has upon the seas and always provides the same amount of oxygen. Though man dumps a tremendous amount of carbon dioxide into the atmosphere, this is absorbed into the ocean and man is able to continue to live on this planet. If the atmosphere were not as thick as it is, we would be crushed by the billions of pieces of cosmic debris and meteorites that fall continually upon our planet.

Then there is the amazing nitrogen cycle. Nitrogen is extremely inert—if it were not, we would all be poisoned by different forms of nitrous combinations. However, because of its inertness, it is impossible for us to get it to combine naturally with other things. It is definitely needed for plants in the ground. What provision does God make to get the nitrogen out of the air into the soil? He does so by lightning! One hundred thousand lightning bolts strike this planet daily, creating a hundred million tons of usable nitrogen plant food in the soil every year.

Forty miles up there is a thin layer of ozone. If compressed it would be only a quarter of an inch thick, and yet without it life could not exist. Eight killer rays fall upon this planet continually from the sun; without ozone we would be burned, blinded, and broiled by them in just a day or two. The ultraviolet rays come in two forms: longer rays, which are deadly and are screened out, and shorter rays, which are necessary for life on earth and are admitted by the ozone layer. Furthermore, the most deadly of these rays are allowed through the ozone layer in just a very thin amount, enough to kill the green algae, which otherwise would grow to fill all the lakes, rivers, and oceans of the world.

How little we realize what God is continuously doing to provide for our lives. We see that we live with a tiny ozone layer protecting us from an unseen deadly bombardment that constantly comes down upon our heads. Beneath us is a thin rock crust, thinner than the skin of an apple in comparison. Beneath that is the molten lava that forms the core of this earth. So man lives between the burning, blackening rays above and that molten lava below, either of which would burn him to a crisp. Yet man is totally oblivious that God has so arranged things that humans can exist in such a world as this.

Then we have the wonder of water. Nowhere else in the universe do we find water in any abundance except here on the earth. Water, the amazing solvent, dissolves almost everything upon this earth except those things that are life-sustaining.

This amazing liquid exists as ice, breaks up rocks, and produces soil. As snow, it stores up water in the valleys. As rain, it waters and cleanses the earth. As vapor, it provides moisture for much of the arable land of this earth. It exists as cloud cover, in just the right amount. If we had clouds like Venus, Earth could not exist. But we have exactly 50 percent of the surface of the earth covered by clouds at any one time, allowing just the right amount of sunlight to come through. As steam, it runs the powerful machinery that we have here on the earth. Other than bismuth it is the only liquid that is heavier at 4°C. than it is at freezing. If this were not so, life could not exist on this planet. Therefore, when it is frozen, it is lighter and it rises. If this were not so, lakes and rivers would freeze from the bottom up and kill all fish. The algae would be destroyed, and our oxygen supply would cease, and mankind would die.

Even dust provides an incredible function for mankind. If it were not for dust, we would never see a blue sky. Seventeen miles above this planet there is no dust from the earth, and the sky is always black. If it were not for dust, it would never rain. One drop of rain is made up of eight million droplets of water, and each one of those eight million droplets is wrapped around a tiny particle of dust. Without these, the world would become parched and life would cease to exist.

Within human beings, there are many things that tell us we have been made by God. Our life is based upon the blood that flows in our veins. The amazing red blood cell, created in the bone marrow, immediately gives up its nucleus when it reaches the bloodstream. For any other cell, this would mean death, like cutting the heart right out of a man. A red blood cell is formed like a doughnut with a thin membrane across the hole. Without a nucleus it is able to carry more oxygen for the body because of this membrane and the shape of the cell. If it were shaped like other cells, it would require nine times as many cells to provide oxygen for the human body.

Then there is that wonder of wonders: the human eye! How could anybody look at a human eye and suppose that it just happened? Evolutionists tell us that where there is want, nature will provide what is needed. Can you imagine that we needed sight? No one had ever seen anything, but there was a need to see something. So nature created an eye. Imagine creating two eyes on a horizontal plane so that we can not only see but also have a range finder that determines distances.

Did you ever wonder what happens to your tears that continually flow across your eyes? Dr. William Paley wrote a classic work titled *Natural Theology* in which he discusses the eye. "In order to keep the eye moist and clean—which qualities are necessary to its brightness and its use—a wash is constantly supplied by a secretion for the purpose; and the superfluous brine is conveyed to the nose through a perforation in the bone as large as a goose quill. When once the fluid has entered the nose, it spreads itself upon the inside of the nostril and is evaporated by the current of warm air which in the course of respiration is continually passing over it. . . . It is easily perceived that the eye must want moisture; but could the want of the eye generate the gland which produces the tear, or bore the hole by which it is discharged—a hole through a bone?"[7] Let the atheist or the evolutionist tell us who bored the hole in the bone and laid a water pipe through it for the dispersion of our tears.

Sir Charles Scott Sherrington, famous English physiologist of Oxford who wrote a classic work on the eye, said: "Behind the intricate mechanism of the human eye lie breathtaking glimpses of a Master Plan."[8] When confronted with darkness the human eye increases its ability to see one hundred thousand times. The finest camera ever made does not even vaguely approach such a thing, but the human eye does it automatically. Furthermore, the eye will find the object it wants to see and focus upon it automatically. It will elongate or compress itself. Both eyes moving together must take different angles to fix themselves upon what is to be seen. When the eye got ready to create itself, it also had the forethought for its own protection and built itself beneath the bony ridge of the brow, and also provided a nose on which to hang the glasses that most of us need. Then it provided a shutter to protect itself from any foreign object.

Last, we might mention the incredible mind of man. Sir Henry Fairfield Osborn, the noted modern anthropologist, said: "To my mind, the human brain is the most marvelous and mysterious object in the whole universe." Weighing but 3.3 pounds, it can perform what 500 tons of electrical and electronic equipment cannot do. Containing 10 to 15 billion neurons, each a living unit in itself, it performs feats that absolutely boggle the mind.[9] Dr. H. M. Morris said: "Therefore, men who reject or ignore God do so, not because science or reason requires them to, but purely and simply because they want to!"[10]

The Scripture says, "And even as they did not like to

retain God in their knowledge, God gave them over to a reprobate mind" (Romans 1:28).

Not only are these compelling reasons for the existence of God, but I believe in God because I believe in Jesus Christ. The prophecies, the birth, the life, the miracles, the teachings, the death, and the resurrection of Jesus Christ, and His continuous performance of those things He said He would do convince me that God lives and that God lived in Jesus Christ and even now can transform people.

In his best-selling book *Through the Valley of the Kwai*, Ernest Gordon told about American soldiers captured by the Japanese in the Malay Peninsula who were tortured and starved. They were turned into a group of animals, clawing and fighting and stealing food from one another. Finally things became so bad they decided to start reading the New Testament. As Gordon, a university graduate, read those words to them from the New Testament, these men were converted to the living God through Jesus Christ. This community of animals was transformed into a community of love because God lives and He lives in Jesus Christ. Christ is willing to live in the hearts of those who will trust in Him. This joy, this peace, this transformed life, and this assurance of eternal life are what Christ offers to those who will place their trust in His atoning death.

"The heart is a God-shaped blank, and only God can fill it." That maxim has been around for more than 1,700 years. Today there are millions of people who are trying to fill their hearts with everything except God and they do not succeed. What an incredible truth—only God can fill it. You cannot run a jet plane on tomato juice, and you cannot fill the God-shaped blank of the human heart created by Him, for Him, with anything else at all.

I remember when Dr. Manford George Gutzke, one of my professors during my seminary days, told us that a woman once asked him an interesting question.

"My six-year-old daughter wants to know who created God. What should I tell her?"

"Just tell her that nobody created God; He has always existed and will always exist," he told the woman.

"But she is only six years old. She won't understand that."

"That's all right," said Dr. Gutzke. "When she gets to be sixty years old, she still won't understand it, but you tell her anyway, because it's the truth."

We cannot wrap our minds around the infinite God or we would be greater than He is. We can apprehend Him, but we cannot comprehend Him entirely.

Have you heard of Pascal's famous wager? Pascal, who lived a couple of hundred years ago in France, was a great Christian theologian, mathematician, and scholar. One day he was talking to an unbeliever. He told the man, "If I am wrong about God existing, then neither of us would ever know it, because we would both die and cease to exist, and all consciousness would disappear. But, on the other hand, if I am right and you are wrong, when we both die, I will go to heaven and you will go to hell. Now," he added, "it seems to me that any intelligent man would bet on the right side of that wager."

What does the unbeliever have to offer? Such an unbeliever, W. O. Saunders, wrote in the *American Magazine:* "I would like to introduce you to one of the lonesomest and unhappiest individuals on earth. I am talking about the man who does not believe in God. I can introduce you to such a man because I myself am one, and in introducing myself, you shall have an introduction to the agnostic or skeptic in your own neighborhood, for he is everywhere in the land. You will be surprised to learn that the agnostic envies your faith in God, your settled belief in a heaven after life, and your blessed assurance that you will meet with your loved ones in an afterlife where there will be neither sadness nor pain. He would give anything to be able to embrace that faith and be comforted by it. For him there is only the grave and the persistence of matter. After the grave all he can see is the disintegration of the protoplasm and psychoplasm of which my body and personality are composed. But in this materialist view, I find neither ecstasy nor happiness.

"The agnostic may face life with a smile and a heroic attitude. He may put on a brave front, but he is not happy. He stands in awe and reverence before the vastness and majesty of the universe, knowing not whence he came nor why. He is appalled at the stupendousness of space and the infinitude of time, humiliated by the infinite smallness of himself, cognizant of his own frailty, weakness, and brevity. Certainly he sometimes yearns for a staff on which to lean. He, too, carries a cross. For him, this earth is but a tricky raft adrift in the unfathomable waters of eternity with no horizon in sight. His heart aches for every precious life upon the raft—drifting, drifting, drifting, whither no one knows."[11]

Quite a few years ago, I was invited to debate an atheist on a radio talk show. The first thing I asked this well-educated unbeliever was, "Do you deny the existence of God?"

"Absolutely," he answered.

"Wonderful," I said. "I suppose you understand that atheism is irrational."

"What do you mean? Of course not," countered the atheist because atheists pride themselves above everything as being quite rational, indeed, in fact more rational than the rest of the believing world.

"Oh yes, it is," I answered. "Atheism is a universal negative. Everyone who has studied logic knows that you cannot prove a universal negative." I reminded him that if you say there is no such thing in the entire universe as little green men, for instance, there is no way to prove it. You'd have to travel through every planet and every star and inside every star and through every galaxy in the entire universe and come back and tell me that you didn't see one. When you did, I could just answer, "Well, you missed him. While you were going that way, he was zigging this way." To prove little green men don't exist you'd have to examine every single part of the universe *at the same time.* So it's impossible to prove that there is no such thing as little green men or angels or God. Therefore atheism is a logical contradiction, and to affirm a logical contradiction is irrational.

"So, sir," I told the atheist, "you are an irrational man." So is the concept of a world without a Creator, and a human heart that does not yearn for a God to fill it.

I believe in God. However, to believe in Him is not enough, for even the devil believes in God and trembles. It is necessary not only that we believe He exists but also that we believe He became incarnate in Jesus Christ and that He died for our sins. It is necessary that we believe and that we repent of our sins and cast ourselves at His feet and place our trust in Him—in His atoning death for our salvation. If not, we shall face Him as our angry Judge in that great day. I believe in Him, and I know He is alive. He lives in my heart, and He has granted me the assurance that I shall live with Him forever. It is my earnest desire that that assurance may be yours, if it is not already. Have *you* trusted in Him?

CHAPTER FOUR

WHY I BELIEVE IN CREATION

In the beginning God created the heaven and the earth.

GENESIS 1:1

Examining creation will bring us closer to the Creator. That is what the earliest founders of science believed, or as the founder of astronomy put it, we would be merely thinking God's thoughts after Him.

But something happened on the way to the twentieth century. In the middle of the nineteenth century when modern science began to develop, the entire scientific enterprise was hijacked.

I am referring to Darwin's theory of evolution. Canada's leading scientist, who was chosen to write the Introduction to the centennial edition of *The Origin of the Species,* said that the greatest evil Darwin has brought upon the world is to somehow divide science from God and, in fact, set the two at each other's throats.

The theory of evolution has had enormous and devastating impact upon the modern world in which we live. Michael Denton, author of a fascinating book titled *Evolution: A Theory in Crisis,* wrote:

> The voyage on *The Beagle* [Darwin's ship on which he set sail from England in 1831] was a journey of awesome significance. Its object was to survey Patagonia; its result was to shake the foundations of western thought. *The Origin of the Species* [which followed] has been referred to as "one of the most important books ever written" [it is because it seeks to shake the foundation of the most important book ever written]. As far as Christianity was concerned, the advent of the theory of evolution and the elimination of traditional teleological thinking was catastrophic.

Teleological thinking is the thinking you and I engage in every day. To think teleologically is to believe life has purpose and an end. The evolutionist believes nothing has purpose or an end. Consequently, life has no significance or meaning or importance. The whole scientific enterprise, however, has been hijacked into a naturalistic or materialistic view of the world. Naturalism believes that there is nothing in the universe but nature, nothing supernatural; materialism believes that there is nothing in the world but matter.

What does that mean? It means that we live in a time when there are only two religions competing for the minds, hearts, and loyalties of Western man. The future of this world will be determined, humanly speaking, by Western man. One of those religions is Christianity; the other religion is evolution. Anyone who does not realize that evolution is a religion does not know much about evolution. It is a religion that is passionately held by its devotees. Listen to what some well-known evolutionists, all highly placed scientists in the world, have to say. Professor Louis T. More, one of the most vocal evolutionists: "The more one studies paleontology [the fossil record], the more certain one becomes that evolution is based on faith alone."[1] Professor D. M. S. Watson, a famous evolutionist, made the remarkable observation that evolution itself is a theory universally accepted, "not because it has been observed to occur or can be proved by logically coherent evidence to be true, but because the only alternative—special creation—is clearly incredible."[2] To the reprobate mind, the unregenerate mind, creation is incredible because it requires belief in a creator, and that is totally unacceptable to such men as these. A famous British evolutionist, Sir Arthur Keith, is just as frank in his admission. He says, "Evolution is unproved and unprovable. We believe it because the only alternative is special creation, which is unthinkable."[3]

What would happen if I were to stand up before my congregation and say, "My friends, Christianity is unproved and unprovable but still you ought to believe it"? They would get up and walk out, and rightly so. But that is the way men accept evolution—by blind faith!

Yet over and over again in our colleges' textbooks, evolution is taught as a proved fact. A modern textbook titled *General Zoology* states, "All scientists at the present time agree that evolution is a fact." This reminds me of the story about a preacher who had his sermon typed out, and written on the side were these words: "Argument weak here. Pound pulpit." So while many scientists may teach that all scientists believe in evolution as proven fact, remember what Sir Arthur Keith said: "Evolution is unproved and unprovable. We believe it because the only alternative is special creation, which is unthinkable." That's an admission of the most blatant prejudice I have ever read. He is saying that scientists are willing to accept a theory that is unproved and unprovable because they are so biased they can't even think about the fact there may be a God who created the world.

A great many people have been led to believe evolution is fact, but it is not. What is it? Professor David Allbrook, professor of anatomy at the University of Western Australia, says that evolution is "a time-honored scientific tenet of faith."[4] Dr. Duane Gish, noted biologist, says, "Evolution is a fairy tale for adults." I believe that is exactly what it is. In *Grimms' Fairy Tales* someone kisses a frog and in two seconds it becomes a prince. That is a fairy tale. In evolution, someone kisses a frog and in two million years it becomes a prince. As Arthur Field has pointed out, evolution is based "upon belief in the reality of the unseen; belief in the fossils that cannot be produced, belief in embryological evidence that does not exist, belief in the breeding experiments that refuse to come off." It is faith—faith in the substance of things unseen. It is a religion. It is the religion of the unbeliever.

Robert T. Clark and James D. Bales wrote an interesting and heavily documented book titled *Why Scientists Accept Evolution*. It contains numerous letters written by Darwin,

Huxley, Spencer, and other early evolutionists. It points out that these men indicated in their letters, by their own admission, that because of their hostility toward God and their bias against the supernatural, they jumped at the doctrine of evolution.[5] Sir Julian Huxley, one of the world's leading evolutionists, head of UNESCO, descendant of Thomas Huxley—"Darwin's bulldog"—said on a talk show, "I suppose the reason we leaped at *The Origin of Species* was because the idea of God interfered with our sexual mores."[6]

Yet, probably the most prevalent reason the average layman believes in evolution—if he does—is that he is told that all scientists believe it. A recent newspaper article, however, indicated that one group of more than five hundred scientists disbelieved it completely, in every single facet. One of the world's leading scientists, Sir Cecil Wakeley, whose credentials are rather impressive—K.B.E., C.B., LL.D., M.CH., Doctor of Science, F.R.C.S., past president of Royal College of Surgeons of Great Britain—said, "Scripture is quite definite that God created the world, and I for one believe that to be a fact, not fiction. There is no evidence, scientific or otherwise, to support the theory of evolution."[7] As famous a scientist as Sir Ambrose Fleming completely rejects evolution, as does the Harvard scientist Louis Agassiz, probably one of the greatest scientists America has produced.

In the first chapter of the Book of Genesis is an amazing statement, coming from thirty-five hundred years ago, of the divine creation of the universe. But it should be pointed out that it is not possible to combine the Bible and evolution, as some people want to do. Surveys show that 40 percent of Americans believe that the Bible is true and evolution is true.

But what many Christians don't realize is the incompatibility and the hostility of evolution toward the Bible and Christianity. Jacque Monod, Nobel prize–winning scientist from France who is an evolutionist and not a Christian, says he is appalled that any Christian would try to embrace evolution. Evolution is the cruelest and most wasteful method of creating man. Instead of God creating us by fiat as the Scripture tells us He did, God, if He used evolution, would have used billions of years and billions of trillions of quadrillions of creatures living and bleeding and dying in order that man might finally appear. So man would have been created on the surface of a gigantic graveyard. That is totally out of sync with any Christian view of God.

No, I believe Christians engage in this compromise only because they think that science has proved evolution, and they must take the Scripture as some sort of putty nose to twist around until they have made it conform to evolution. Those who are evolutionists laugh at the idea that you can put evolution and the Bible together. Thomas Huxley, probably the most famous proponent of evolution who ever lived, stated, "It is clear that the doctrine of evolution is directly antagonistic to that of Creation. . . . Evolution, if consistently accepted, makes it impossible to believe the Bible."[8]

Evolution is the religion of modern unbelieving man, and it has been the pseudoscientific foundation of every false and anti-Christian "ism" that has come down the pike in the last hundred years. For example, consider Nazism. Hitler accepted the evolutionary platitudes of Nietzsche: the idea of a super race. "Preservation of Favoured Races in the Struggle for Life," a subtitle of Darwin's book, had to do with the survival of the fittest race. Hitler's master race was simply an outgrowth of evolutionary thinking. Mussolini, who frequently quoted Darwin in catch phrases, said that the idea of peace was repugnant to the idea of the survival of the fittest and the progress of the race; war was essential for the survival of the fittest.

It is well known that Karl Marx asked Darwin to write the introduction to *Das Kapital* since he felt that Darwin had provided a scientific foundation for communism. Throughout this century, all over the world, those who pushed the communist conspiracy also pushed an evolutionary, imperialistic, naturalistic view of life, endeavoring to crowd the Creator right out of the cosmos.

In the first chapter of Genesis, the Hebrew term *bara*, indicating the direct creation of God, is used three times. It is used, first of all, for the creation of matter—the material cosmos. Second, it is used for the creation of life, and third, for the creation of man.

Every peg upon which evolution has stood is collapsing and crumbling about it today, and more and more scientists are in rebellion. One of France's leading scientists, the author of an eighteen-volume encyclopedia on zoology, whose knowledge of zoology, according to the evolutionist Theodosius Dobzhansky, is absolutely encyclopedic, came out with an attack that demolished evolution on every front. Dobzhansky says that though we may disagree with him, we certainly cannot ignore him, because his knowledge is absolutely staggering. This is interesting because until recently, it has been very difficult for any scientist to make antievolutionary statements in the face of the tremendous pressure that has been exerted upon them.

Let us consider one of the three uses of *bara*, the creation of the material universe. This is a problem that evolutionists never solved. Astronomers believe for the most part a "big bang" theory—once the universe was in one great condensed piece of matter and then it exploded with an explosion beyond our comprehension. It was an explosion that threw out particles the size of the Milky Way, our galaxy. These are speeding outward into space. If true, that would indicate that the universe was not eternal and had a beginning. To overcome this, they said it would slow down and finally come to a stop. Then gravity would pull it back together again, and it would oscillate back and forth throughout all eternity, re-creating itself.

What has science to say about that? An article in the science section of *Time* magazine said concerning the infinite universe: "After years of study and calculation, two respected California astronomers, Allan Sandage and James Gunn, made separate but similar announcements: The universe will continue to expand forever." Sandage, of the Hale Observatories, basing his conclusion on fifteen years of careful observations of distant galaxies, notes that measurements of the amount their light has shifted toward the red end of the spectrum indicates they are not slowing down at all but accelerating. So there is no possibility that these will ever turn back. Even more important, the red shift measurements of nearby galaxies gave no indication of the slightest gravitational slowdown in the outward rush of the galaxies. "It's a terrible surprise," says Sandage, who for years had been a leading proponent of the idea that the universe would eventually close in on itself.

Gunn and Gustav Tammann, who did their work at the Mount Palomar 200-inch-telescope observatory, say that the arguments for a closed universe are almost "theological in nature."[9] People hold to them passionately because if they give them up, they must then acknowledge a beginning of the universe. Along with a beginning, there must be a creator, a God, to whom they must answer. "This expansion is such a strange conclusion," Gunn said, "that one's first assumption is that it cannot really be true, and yet, it is the premier fact."[10] And for that premier fact of modern astronomy—that the universe had a beginning—the evolutionist now has no explanation whatsoever.

Then consider the creation of life. Darwin repeatedly referred to the simple single cell. With the crude microscopes available in his time, the single cell looked a little bit like a tiny basketball with a seed in the middle of it. But now the human cell is known to be fantastically complex, made up of hundreds of thousands of smaller protein molecules, and Harvard University paleontologist George Gaylord Simpson tells us that a single protein molecule is the most complicated substance known to mankind. A single cell is so infinitely complex that it boggles the minds of scientists who have studied it.

A recent science that has developed is the science of probability. Dr. James Coppedge, Ph.D., director of the Center for Probability Research in Biology in California, applied all the laws of probability studies to the possibility of a single cell coming into existence by chance. He considered in the same way a single protein molecule, and even a single gene. His discoveries are revolutionary. He computed a world in which the entire crust of the earth—all the oceans, all the atoms, and the whole crust were available. He then had these amino acids bind at a rate one and one-half trillion times faster than they do in nature. In computing the possibilities, he found that to provide a single protein molecule by chance combination would take 10,262 years. Most of us do not have any idea what that means. To get a single cell—the single smallest living cell known to mankind—which is called the mycroplasm hominis H 39, would take 10,119,841 years. That means that if you took thin pieces of paper and wrote one and then wrote zeros after them, you would fill up the entire known universe with paper before you could ever even write that number. That is how many years it would take to make one living cell, one smaller than any human cell!

In trying to explain to us the length of time it would take for chance to produce one usable gene, Dr. Coppedge suggested that we imagine a single amoeba trying to carry the entire known universe one atom at a time across the entire width of the universe (which astronomers estimate to be thirty billion light-years). At what speed would this energetic and never-dying one-celled animal carry out this stupendous task? Dr. Coppedge reduced its speed to the slowest conceivable speed, namely, one angstrom unit every fifteen billion years. This means that the amoeba would be traveling the width of the smallest known atom, the hydrogen atom, in the supposed entire time that the universe has existed; that is, fifteen billion years. At this incredibly slow speed, how long would it take our super-persistent amoeba to move the entire universe over the width of one universe? The time requirements for such a transgalactic job are mind-boggling. However, before one usable gene could be produced by chance, our indefatigable amoeba would not only have moved the entire universe one atom at a time, but it would also have moved more universes than the four billion people living on this planet could count if every one of them counted twenty-four hours a day as fast as they could for the next five thousand years. Yet evolutionists would have us believe that things vastly more complex than this happen all the time.[11]

Emile Borel, the great French scientist and probability expert, points out that if anything on the cosmic level is of a probability ratio of more than 1050 to 1, it will never happen. The probability of producing a human cell by chance is 10,119,000 to 1, a number we cannot even comprehend. According to the probability scientists, it could never happen. The same is true with all other development, including man's. We are told that somehow in the last two billion years, not only did this come to pass, but this single living cell also evolved into every other kind of living creature—that all living beings evolved from that one single thing.[12]

Thomas Huxley said: "The primary and direct evidence in favor of evolution can be furnished only by paleontology. . . . If evolution has taken place, its marks will be left; if it has not taken place, there will be its refutation."[13] The great evolutionist says that it is only in paleontology—only in the fossil record—that evolution will be proved.

"Geological research . . . does not yield the infinitely many fine gradations between past and present species required."[14] The author of that statement was Charles Darwin.

George Gaylord Simpson of Harvard, the high priest of evolution today, stated, "In spite of these examples, it remains true, as every paleontologist knows, that most new species, genera, and families, and that nearly all categories above the level of families, appear in the record suddenly and are not led up to by known, gradual, completely continuous transitional sequences."[15] We know that in the Cambrian strata of rock, all the invertebrate animals in the world suddenly appear completely complex creatures with no ancestors before them, which is totally inexplicable to the evolutionists.

A scientist by the name of Richard Goldschmidt points out that it is impossible by micromutations to form any new species. He said in his book *Theoretical Genetics*, "It is true that nobody thus far has produced a new species, or genus, etc., by macromutation. It is equally true that nobody has produced even a species by the selection of micromutations." In fact, he so abandons the possibility of ever slowly forming new species that he is led to what he calls his "hopeful monster theory."[16] The hopeful monster theory is simply that one day a lizard laid an egg and sat on it and hatched an eagle!

If you think that is amazing, a scientist by the name of Geoffrey Bourne recently stated that his examination of men and apes has led him to the definite conclusion that apes evolved from men. Another scientist, B. C. Nelson, examining the similarities in blood between various animals, has concluded that a pig is the closest relative to a human being—not an ape.[17] If those differing conclusions can be drawn from the same evidence, what kind of evidence is being looked at?

Professor Enoch, zoologist at the University of Madras, said: "The facts of paleontology seem to support creation and the flood rather than evolution. For instance, *all the major groups of invertebrates appear 'suddenly'* in the first fossiliferous strata (Cambrian) of the earth with their distinct specializations indicating that they were all created almost at the same time."[18]

The vocal evolutionist T. H. Morgan said in his book, *Evolution and Adaptation*: "Within the period of human history we do not know of a single instance of the transformation of one species into another one. . . . It may be claimed that the theory of descent is lacking, therefore, in the most essential feature that it needs to place the theory on a scientific basis. This must be admitted." Not a single instance, and yet Huxley claims that if the evidence isn't there, it is nowhere to be found.

It is not there! Some of the greatest scientists in the world look upon evolution as something absolutely absurd, impossible, and unprovable. Yet millions accept it because they have been brainwashed into thinking it is true.

The truth is that *God* made you and me. Those who carried away the scientific movement created by Christians to draw us closer to God, and who have postulated a naturalistic, materialistic, atheistic world and have indoctrinated hundreds of millions of students in it all over the world, have been at last found out for what they are—they have been teachers of falsehoods and they have promulgated the "Great Lie."

Hundreds of books and articles have been written in the last decades of the twentieth century that point out that evolution is falling apart, that there are fissures appearing in the walls and floor, that the columns have collapsed. There is going to be a revolution in thinking, and evolution will come to be thought of as merely a small cult of the twentieth century—a sect.

Arthur Denton wrote, "The suggestion that life and man are the result of chance is incompatible with the biblical assertion of their being the direct result of intelligent creative activity. It was because Darwinian theory broke man's link with God and set him adrift in a cosmos without purpose or end that its impact was so fundamental."

The impact, though, will not last. Traditional teleological thinking—that there is purpose to life and a meaningful end—will triumph and continue to rule our days on earth. There is purpose in our lives and there will be an end. "Fearfully and wonderfully made . . ." That is what King David declared we all are, an extraordinarily wonderfully wrought creation, "and my soul knoweth right well."

One day we will give an account to Him of our lives. The Scripture plainly declares that all of us have transgressed His law and are culpable in His sight and when we come before Him, if we are judged according to our merits, we will be condignly condemned forever. This means that we have no hope except in His mercy and that mercy has been manifested in Jesus Christ, His Son, whom He sent into this world to live in our place and die in our stead. His Word declares that if we will place our trust in Christ, He will freely forgive us our sins and give us the gift of eternal life. One day we will stand before our Creator. If we are trusting in some supposed goodness, morality, piety, or religiosity in ourselves, we will not make it. Let us flee to the cross to be clothed in the righteousness of Christ that we may stand faultless before our Creator.

CHAPTER FIVE

WHY I BELIEVE IN HEAVEN

And I heard a great voice out of heaven saying,
Behold, the tabernacle of God is with men, and he
will dwell with them, and they shall be his people, and
God himself shall be with them, and be their God.
And God shall wipe away all tears from their eyes;
and there shall be no more death, neither sorrow, nor
crying, neither shall there be any more pain: for the
former things are passed away.

REVELATION 21:3–4

No question has plagued the minds of men and women more continuously and universally than the question raised by Job so many centuries ago. The earliest book of the Old Testament echoes forth that question that has been wrenched from the hearts of innumerable people ever since: from a husband and wife as, with clenched hands, they have looked down on the cold face of their little child in a casket; from comrades as they have looked down at the shattered body of a soldier in arms. In every family where there is an empty chair, the question has been inescapably wrung from their hearts, in the words of Job: "If a man die, shall he live again?" (14:14).

More than thirteen hundred years ago in the portion of England known as Northumbria, the first Christian missionaries arrived. They came to the courts of King Edwin of Northumbria, and in his great hall ablaze with the light of many torches, huge logs in the fireplace, and grizzled chieftains surrounding them, these Christian missionaries gave their first discourse on the Christian faith. When they had finished, one asked, "Can this new religion tell us anything of what happens after death? The soul of man is like a sparrow flying through this lighted hall. It enters at one door from the darkness outside, flits through the light and warmth, and passes out at the further end into the dark again. Can this new religion solve for us the mystery?"[1]

I, for one, am convinced that this new religion, now old with age, is the only one that can give us any sure and certain word concerning life after death. I believe in immortality; I believe in heaven. The reasons are manifold. Not all of them have the same weights in my mind or the minds of any other individuals, of course, but together they form the threads of what I believe is an exceedingly strong cord.

First of all, let us consider an argument from the realm of science. The first law of thermodynamics states that energy or matter cannot be created or destroyed. They may be transformed one into the other, but they cannot be destroyed. This was set forth by Einstein and was conclusively demonstrated at Hiroshima. Burris Jenkins put it this way: "No single atom in creation can go out of existence, according to the scientists; it only changes in form. We cannot burn up anything; we simply change it from a solid to a gaseous state. Neither is any energy or force ever destroyed; it is only changed from one form to another."[2] If man ceases to exist, he will be the only thing in this universe that does. Therefore, to begin with, there is the probability that we shall continue to exist.

Second, let us consider this analogy from nature. It has probably never been stated any better than by William Jennings Bryan in his *Analogies of Nature:* "Christ gave us proof of immortality, and yet it would hardly seem necessary that one should rise from the dead to convince us that the grave is not the end. If the Father deigns to touch with Divine power the cold and pulseless heart of the buried acorn and to make it burst forth into a new life, will He leave neglected in the earth the soul of man, made in the image of his Creator? If He stoops to give to the rosebush whose withered blossoms float upon the autumn breeze, the sweet assurance of another springtime, will He refuse the words of hope to the sons of men when the frosts of winter come? If matter, mute and inanimate, though changed by the forces of nature into a multitude of forms, can never die, will the spirit of man suffer annihilation when it has paid a brief visit like a royal guest to this tenement of clay? No, I am as sure that there is another life as I am that I live today!"[3]

Third, there is the universal longing of mankind for eternity. Some people may never have considered that such a longing does not exist in the breast of any part of the brute creation. In his book *After Death—What?* Dr. Madison C. Peters said: "The flocks and herds upon a thousand hills, the myriad forms of insect life, every winged fly and tuneful beetle, the fish that gaily sport and gambol in the rivers and seas, all can find the end of their being; not a thought of future want disturbs their perfect tranquility. But never so with man. He only is never satisfied no matter what his wealth or fame or knowledge or power or earthly pleasures. From the king to the beggar, 'man never is, but always to be blest.'"

What is the explanation? I believe the Scriptures give to us very clearly the fact that God has placed immortality— eternity—in the breast of man. He only of all of God's creation longs for eternal life. This longing is found everywhere. It is a universal experience of mankind that forbids him to accept any other answer to the riddle of life. Emerson said, "The blazing evidence of immortality is our dissatisfaction with any other solution."[4]

Wherever men have gone in the world, they have found certain innate ideas in the human heart and mind. They do not arise from experience; they are there, inbred, and these innate ideas are the corresponding human ideas to the instincts of animals. What are they? There is everywhere a belief in God. There is everywhere a belief in right and wrong. There is a belief in cause and effect. There is a belief in time and space. And there is universally found a belief in immortality. There have been some who have denied this. Dr. Edwards made an exhaustive search to try to find some tribe, however remote, that did not have some belief in immortality. That belief may be distorted; it may be but a dim reflection of the glory that really is; but nevertheless, however perverted or distorted, every instance he found in which some group appeared not to believe in immortality dissolved in the light of further examination.

There has never been a race of men upon this earth—whether in the deepest heart of Africa, in the South Seas, or on the highest mountain—that has not had a belief in some future life, whether it is the happy hunting grounds of the American Indians, some palace in the sky, some sensual abode of the Muslim. What is the explanation? Long before the evidence for this universal belief had been collected, Cicero said this: "In everything the consent of all nations is to be accounted the law of nature, and to resist it is to resist the voice of God."[5]

This has been true not only of the brute savage, the superstitious, and the ignorant but also of the greatest philosophical minds of history. Crito asked Socrates on the night of the latter's death: "But in what way would you have us bury you?" "In any way that you like," Socrates replied, "only you must get hold of me, and take care that I do not walk away from you." Plato, in his *Phaedon*, presents powerful arguments for a belief in immortality, as do the philosopher Schelling and others too numerous to be mentioned.[6]

Other authors and poets, such as Thomas Carlyle, Thomas Jefferson, Heinrich Heine, also voice the theme. Goethe put it this way: "How strongly we may be chained and attached to this earth, by thousands and thousands of appearances, a certain intimate longing compels us to lift up our eyes to heaven; because a deep inexplicable feeling gives us the conviction that we are citizens of another world, which shines above us." Alfred Lord Tennyson said:

For tho' from out our bourne of Time and Place
The flood may bear me far,

I hope to see my Pilot face to face
When I have crost the bar.[7]

Byron said this:

I feel my immortality o'ersweep
All pains, all tears, all fears, and peal,
Like the eternal thunders of the deep,
Into my ears this truth—"Thou liv'st for ever!"[8]

Everywhere, from the Fiji Islands to the dens of the philosophers, it has been believed that man shall live on. Addison has summed up man's confidence of eternal life:

The soul secured in her existence, smiles
    at the drawn dagger, and defies its point.
The stars shall fade away, the sun himself
Grow dim with age, and nature sink in years,
But thou shalt flourish in immortal youth,
Unhurt amidst the wars of elements,
The wrecks of matter, and the crush of worlds.[9]

We have been made for eternity! Yet though such a belief exists in every ancient religion from the Egyptian to the Persian to the Assyrian and Babylonian, the Chinese and the Hindu, everywhere it has waited for Jesus Christ to give to it a certitude nothing else could grant.

Professor Adolf von Harnack said: "Christ's grave was the birthplace of an indestructible belief that death is vanquished and there is life eternal. It is useless to cite Plato; it is useless to point to the Persian religion and the ideas and literature of later Judaism. All that would have perished; but the certainty of the resurrection and of a life eternal which is bound up with the grave in Joseph's garden has not perished; and on the conviction that Jesus lives we still base those hopes of citizenship in an Eternal City which make our earthly life worth living and tolerable. He delivered them who, through tear of death, were all their lifetime subject to bondage."[10] "He is risen" is the certain and sure hope of all those who trust in Him. Not only do we have the universal testimony of mankind, but we also have the testimony of Jesus Christ and His resurrection.

Dr. Simon Greenleaf, the Royal Professor of Law at Harvard, one of the greatest authorities on legal evidence the world has ever known, turned the vast searchlight of his immense knowledge of evidences upon the evidence for the resurrection of Jesus Christ and exposed every thread of that evidence to the most searching criticism. He came to the conclusion that the evidence was so overwhelming that in any unbiased courtroom in the world it would be declared to be a historical fact.

Every shred of evidence for the resurrection of Christ is evidence for eternal life in heaven. For that same Jesus said: "I am he that liveth, and was dead; and, behold, I am alive for evermore. . . . Because I live ye shall live also. . . . I go to prepare a place for you" (Revelation 1:18; John 14:19; 14:2).

We should also consider that the evidence for the inspiration of the Scriptures is a revelation from God. It is also evidence for the fact of eternal life. Those evidences themselves are so powerful that they cannot be gainsaid. Never has a skeptic been able to overturn or overthrow the evidences for the inspiration of the Scriptures. Those evidences are also further support for the fact of eternal life in heaven, for those same Scriptures declare most assuredly that those who trust in Christ shall live forever. Remember also that evidence for God is evidence for eternal life. Every one of those evidences is also another pillar for the great doctrine of eternal life. For that God who made us to dwell "for a few moments in this tenement of clay" would not delude us. None of us has even begun to develop the talents God has given. No one knows even the smallest fraction of that realm of life or nature or art that he has taken upon himself to study. The more we learn, the more we see that we have only touched the fringe of the garment—that God has given us all eternity in which to develop those talents.

Another evidence is that of dying. In my library there are a number of books containing within them the last words of thousands of famous people when they came to the place of death. One thing is absolutely clear—those who believed in Jesus Christ died in a way remarkably different from those who did not. An unbelieving psychiatrist heard the evidences for the resurrection of Christ presented. This man said that he had "seen enough people die to know that there is a difference between an evangelical Christian dying and anyone else."

One can see it in the writings of last words. On one page of a book on how we face death we find the words of a noted infidel, Edward Gibbon—"All is dark." Another page gives us the last words of Augustus Toplady, author of the hymn "Rock of Ages": "All is light, light, light!"[11]

Thousands and thousands of people have been granted some presentiment of that which was to come. They have seen a foretaste of the glory that was theirs; they have seen those who have died and gone before, and in those final minutes before they left this world, heaven opened up before them and gave them a vision of the world to which they were about to go. For others, hell also has opened its mouth to swallow them. "Demons are in the room and are about to pull me down," cried the infidel Adams. The final words of the most famous of this world's skeptics and atheists are enough to make your blood run cold.

Newer evidence that goes even further has been given to us by Dr. Elisabeth Kübler-Ross and Dr. Raymond Moody, two psychiatrists. When Dr. Kübler-Ross first presented to the world the evidences of her studies, she described herself as a nonreligious person. This woman, considered by many the world's leading authority on death and dying, has attended thousands upon thousands of terminally ill patients. In her work she began to encounter the phenomenon of people pronounced clinically dead who were resuscitated—at first two or three, then more and more. Between them, she and Dr. Moody have examined more than five hundred people who have died and come back.

These people have described either a place of beauty, wonder, joy, and peace, or they have described something terrible. These people have floated out of their bodies, and though out of their bodies they had bodies that were real, and though blind they could see while they were called "dead" by doctors. They tell about who came into the room, what those persons looked like, and what they did. Yet when they were brought back, the blind could not see. A doctor told me of his experience in attending a man who had been pronounced clinically dead. He succeeded in resuscitating the man, who then sued the doctor for bringing him back into this miserable existence from the glory he had experienced. One woman, describing her situation after she had suffered a respiratory arrest, said the doctors who were trying to resuscitate her were pounding on her body trying to get her back while she was over them, looking down, and saying, "Leave me alone!"[12] There was such peace, wholeness, happiness, joy, and love as they had never experienced before—an evidence perhaps God has given in these unbelieving days to convict even the most skeptical.

Today, with the advent of cardiopulmonary resuscitation, commonly known as CPR, literally millions of people world-wide have been dead and have come back to life. I have talked to those who have been to heaven and to hell, and both are as real to them as this world is real to us.

I have even recorded the experience of a man who went to hell. I asked him later, "Do you believe there's a hell?"

"No," he answered, "I don't believe there's a hell. I know there's a hell, and I don't plan to go back there again."

My friends, I am convinced there is a life after this! Life goes on; it does not cease. The question is not whether a man shall live again if he die, for we most certainly will die and most certainly will live again. The question is where we will spend eternity—for on this train of life, there is more than one station. For though there is a heaven, which the Bible abundantly makes clear, it makes it equally plain that not everybody is going there. Listen to the words of Jesus: "Enter ye in at the strait gate: for wide is the gate, and broad is the way, that leadeth to destruction, and many there be which go in thereat: Because strait is the gate, and narrow is the way, which leadeth unto life, and few there be that find it" (Matthew 7:13–14).

I have in my library numbers of books crammed full with nothing but the last words of famous people, and one thing I've noticed is that the final words of the unbeliever are vastly different from the final words of believers in Christ. Even an unbelieving doctor, who had sat by the bedsides of numerous people, once said, "There is a vast difference between the death of an evangelical Christian and all other people."

We will live forever, somewhere! For some it will be in the bliss and felicity of heaven, where the mind of man and the heart of man never have conceived what glories God has prepared for those that love and trust Him. Others will live never-endingly in hell! Ignore it, laugh at it, repress it, suppress it, but this will happen nonetheless!

How then does one go to heaven? Thomas said, "Lord, we know not whither thou goest; and how can we know the way?" (John 14:5). So many follow in Thomas's train, not knowing the way. Jesus answered him, "I am the way, the truth, and the life: no man cometh unto the Father, but by me" (v. 6).

The way to heaven is as narrow as the cross. Only those who are willing to humble themselves and acknowledge their sin and place their trust in the Son of God who died in their stead will ever enter the gates of heaven. There are two personal truths I know about myself. The first is: I ought to go to hell because that is where I belong. In ten thousand times, in ten thousand ways, in word and thought, omission and commission, I have transgressed the holy law of God. I stand guilty before God, condignly deserving His just displeasure. But the second truth, which I know equally, is that I am going to heaven because Jesus Christ went to hell on a cross for me. I have no other hope but Him and His free gift. "Let him take the water of life freely" (Revelation 22:17).

CHAPTER SIX

WHY I BELIEVE
IN HELL

*And whosoever was not found written in the book of
life was cast into the lake of fire.*

REVELATION 20:15

W hy I believe in hell! No subject in the world is so repugnant to the human mind as this one, yet no subject is of greater importance.

Jesus wept when He contemplated the destruction of Jerusalem. God Himself says, "I have no pleasure in the death of the wicked" (Ezekiel 33:11). No Christian can find joy in the contemplation of the final abode of the impenitent. However, it is our duty as faithful ministers of Jesus Christ to proclaim the whole counsel of God. I believe I would be a false friend to any sinners if I did not warn them, as the Scriptures repeatedly do, of the danger of their condition.

It is a well-known fact that people suppress what they hate and fear. Consequently there are numerous persons who, instead of seriously considering the matter of hell, simply castigate the one who brings it to their attention. Though a minister may have half a dozen degrees, he is still railed upon as an obscurantist who is to be ignored if he preaches on the subject. I have found that the arguments of unbelievers consist of one thing: emotionalism, displayed in an outburst of hostility and unwillingness to consider rationally a matter of the greatest importance to their eternal well-being.

Some people seem to be under the delusion that hell has evaporated, or at least that all intelligent people have stopped believing in it. Before continuing in any such ideas, I ask you to consider these words of the great Princeton theologian, A. A. Hodge: "The Old Testament was in the hands of the Jews centuries before Christ came. They uniformly understood these Scriptures as teaching that the wicked are to suffer forever." The historian Josephus declares that this was also the understanding of the Pharisees of his time. As Christians we have had Scriptures for almost twenty centuries. We read that "all the great church fathers, Reformers, and historical churches, with their recensions and translations of the Sacred Scriptures, their liturgies and hymns; all the great evangelical theologians and biblical scholars, with their grammars, dictionaries, commentaries, and classical systems, have uniformly agreed in their understanding of the teaching of the Sacred Scriptures as to the endlessness of the future sufferings of all who die impenitent. And this has come to pass against the universal and impetuous current of human fears and sympathies."[1]

The Bible tells us that the unbeliever will go into endless punishment. Is that contrary to what any rational, right-thinking person would conclude from what we know as natural theology, that is, in God's revelation of Himself to us in this world, in the moral government of it, in our own constitution, and nature? By no means! Joseph Stiles points out to us that the laws of our nature demand that there be a hell: "Fix your eye upon the very vilest sinner upon earth. Through death, this instant, pass him up to Heaven—with all his lusts, and lies, and hate, and devilish heart—can he be happy there? By a law of his nature, happiness lies in a correspondence between the mind and its subject. By another law of his nature, misery lies in the opposition between the mind and its object. This unholy heart feels, and must ever feel, the deepest aversion to everything that exists or transpires in holy Heaven."[2]

Our own moral nature requires such a place as hell. The human conscience also demands it. All men feel that there is a difference between virtue and vice, and that in character these are moral opposites. And always we treat them as such: We approve virtue and condemn vice. We reward virtue to promote it and punish vice to suppress it. This is also true in all moral governments of any moral nation—laws have been passed because people know that virtue leads to the happiness of the community.

We see another argument from the life of Jesus Christ and His character. Christ, who came meek and mild to save us from pain and suffering, was the One who talked more about hell than any other person in Scripture. Did this One who is truth incarnate, who is the Holy Son of God, come to implant in the minds of men a fear that would last for more than nineteen centuries of something that is nonexistent? Such a thought is a great smear upon the character of Jesus Christ.

Some people say: "But God is love! And God will never punish anyone in hell." It is very dangerous to erect a doctrine on an inaccurate premise. Indeed the Bible does teach us that God is love, infinitely compassionate love. But the same Bible teaches us that the same God is holy and just and righteous; that He is of purer eyes than to look upon iniquity, and that He will visit our transgressions with the rod and our iniquity with stripes; that He will by no means clear the guilty.

Long before the love of God was fully manifested in the Scripture, the one great thought inculcated in the minds of the Hebrew people was: "Holy, holy, holy, is the LORD of Hosts" (Isaiah 6:3). The very foundation of His throne was holiness, and no sin would ever come into His presence without His inevitably consuming it with His wrath.

There are those who would have us believe that they know something about God that we do not know, and therefore this could not be the case. The Universalist declares that God, in His love, must inevitably receive everyone. This person would boldly approach the Almighty and throw a wing of condescension over the weakness of the Omnipotent God by telling us that God does not quite understand Himself and surely does not mean what He says and actually is gravely mistaken about this matter. This person thinks he knows more about God than God knows about Himself. Here is the blasphemer who would declare that God is some sort of blustering fool who says what He does not mean; that although throughout all of revelation, from Genesis to the end, God declared that the wicked shall die in their sins and not find peace, He now has reversed Himself. This man does not realize that the Scripture says that God's ways are not our ways and His thoughts are not our thoughts (Isaiah 55:8); that His ways and thoughts are past finding out (Romans 11:33). Nevertheless, this blasphemer confidently declares that God's ways *are* our ways and His thoughts *are* our thoughts, and that he has fully found out God's ways. This man would bring upon himself the exclamation of God who has said, in effect, "Mortal, thou supposest that I was altogether such a one as thou art" (Psalm 50:21). He is the Holy God, who has declared that He will not countenance sin. The impenitent thrust themselves into His presence with great folly and with endless consequences.

Others have said, "Surely our sins would not deserve such a thing as endless punishment." Again, let me quote Hodge, the great theologian of Princeton: "We are ourselves the malefactors. It is self-evident that self-interest, that moral blindness and callousness, forever render every criminal an utterly incompetent judge of the measure of guilt attaching to his own wrong-doing. All experience proves this in criminal jurisprudence and in private life. If this be true when we judge of the heinousness of our offenses against our fellow-men, how much more must it vitiate our judgments as to the heinousness of our sins against the infinitely holy God!"[3] Another author has said to us that the end of punishment for our sins must be when the influence of these sins ceases. But if the influences of men's sins live through all time, then men are accountable for those influences through all time. Man cannot but be punished in proportion to his guilt until time be no more. Jesus made it very clear that every human being upon this earth either gathers men and women, boys and girls unto Himself or scatters them abroad. Unbelievers, having spent their whole lives scattering people away from Jesus Christ, will be partly responsible for many of those people ending up in hell.

The Scriptures state that if the effects of our sins are everlasting, then the punishment for our sins will also be everlasting. The main reason we believe in hell is because Jesus Christ declares that it is so. We are told that sinners dwell in "everlasting burnings" (Isaiah 33:14), yet "shall never see light" (Psalm 49:19); are "utterly consumed" (Psalm 73:19), yet "the fire is not quenched" (Mark 9:44); are everlastingly "dead" (Isaiah 26:14); the "worm [in them] dieth not" (Mark 9:44); are torn "in pieces while there is none to deliver" (Psalm 7:2); when they call, they are never answered; when they seek they never find. In a word, they sink to a death beyond prayer, a condemnation beyond forgiveness, and a doom beyond the reach of Christ.

The Hebrew word used in the Old Testament to mean "eternal" is *olam*, along with its cognates and derivatives. In the New Testament the parallel word is the Greek *aion, aionios*, and all of its various cognates, derived from *aei* meaning "always." One author has stated that every Hebrew and Greek word used to describe the eternality of the existence of God and the eternality of the blessedness of the redeemed in heaven is also used to describe the eternality of the sufferings of the lost in hell.[4] If the punishment of the wicked is temporal, then there will come a day when God will be extinct, because the same terms are used. If these terms do not describe eternity, then there is no word in the Hebrew or Greek language that does mean eternity—and this is impossible. Every word that could possibly be used is used.

It would be well for us to consider for a moment the eternality of our souls, which shall dwell either in the bliss and felicity of paradise or in the well-deserved punishment of hell. How long will that be? William Munsey describes to us something of the meaning of *eternity*, something so often men thrust from their minds: "Eternity cannot be defined. Beginningless and endless it cannot be measured—its past increased, its future diminished. It has no past, it has no future, it has no ends, it has no middle, it has no parts—an unanalyzable, tremendous unity. If all the mountains of all the worlds were pressing upon the brain, they could not weigh it down more heavily than eternity's least conception. . . . It is an unoriginated, beginningless, endless, measureless, imperishable, indescribable, undefinable thing. Itself is its only definition. If asked, What is eternity? we can only answer 'Eternity,' and in our answer confess our weakness and folly."[5] It is an infinite circle that can never be measured.

We might conceivably measure the circle of the earth or the circle of our galaxy, or even conceivably the circle of the universe, the great ecliptic that covers the vast spawnings of galaxies around the world. Says Munsey: "Mount Phoebus' solar car, and seat yourself beside the driver, and search for the end of the ecliptic. Lay on the burning whip, and see the fiery-maned and foot-winged steeds dash through the constellations—admiring worlds standing out of your tracks, and space's abysms gaping beneath you; and drive on till the wheels of your car shall shiver, and their worn-out axles break, and the over-driven horses die, and you are lost where no angel will find your bones—and you will find no end to the ethereal circle. But these circles are finite."[6]

Eternity is an infinite circle. Because it is infinite, its center is the great imponderable, portentous "now." "Now" is an infinite circle whose center is everywhere within the compass of that circle. This is boggling to the mind, since it has no circumference and its center is everywhere. "Eternity," says Munsey, "is an infinite line. The strongest winged angel who cleaves the illimitable ether may track it, and track it forever, yet he can no more find its end than he can find the cradle or tomb of God. . . . It is a day without a morning, a day without an evening—an eternal noon. It was just noon when the world was made, it will be just noon when the world is destroyed—high noon forever. O Eternity! The idea deepens, widens, and towers, till the human mind, confounded and crushed, shrinks into infinite littleness."[7] Forever and ever and ever. When you have been in hell a hundred billion, trillion eons of centuries, you will not have one less second to be there—to be lost forever. You will be in utter darkness, fleeing this way and that with never another mortal soul to converse with, never an angel to cross your track, turning this way and that, up and down one plane in every way, forever and ever—lost, lost, shrieking out, lost, forever and ever, where no echoes will ever mock your misery. Immortal soul, lost in an infinite darkness, flying on and on in a journey that will only end when you will come to fold your wings upon the gravestone of God, forever.

Where will you spend forever? Though the Scripture declares it in a thousand places, and Jesus boldly asseverated that it was true, there may be some who still do not believe in hell. I have heard the testimony of a man who went to hell. He is a living man, and his testimony is on tape. He has given me his permission to use it in any way that I wish. He described himself as an atheist. He believed neither in soul nor spirit nor angel nor God. "When you are dead," he said, "you are dead like a dog." One day he planned to crawl into a hole and pull the top in over him. He did not believe in heaven or hell or God.

But then he did, in a very enlightening way—he died! Not long ago he had a cardiac arrest, and the doctors pronounced him clinically dead. (In the last year or so numerous scientists have reported on more than five hundred people who have been pronounced clinically dead and have been resuscitated. Whatever that means, we may not wholly know, but the reports that they bring back have convinced scientists that there is life beyond death.) Later he was resuscitated, but he told me that during his "death" he experienced the following: He sank into a realm of darkness, a place of dark shadows—yet still he had a body. He found himself in great agony pushing a huge stone into a pit. (The Bible speaks of a pit.) He was in great pain, and there was nothing he could do to diminish it.

"If you got shot in the arm," he said, "you could at least grab your arm and get some slight lessening of pain, but not so with this."

I asked, "Where was it? Was it localized?"

His answer was, "No, it was everywhere. I am quite certain that if I had cut my throat I would not have lessened that pain at all."

When I questioned how severe the pain was, he said, "It was worse than anything I have ever experienced in this world."

I thought perhaps he had never known much pain. I

asked, "Have you ever really suffered any pain in this world?"

He said, "Well, when I was nine years old a freight train ran over my leg and left it hanging by a tendon. Somehow I picked it up, dragged myself to a crossing, and was finally picked up by a man in a car. I never passed out, but my blood squirted all over his windshield as he drove me to a hospital. I was never unconscious."

"How did that pain compare to the time when the doctor said you were dead?" I asked.

"It was insignificant," he answered. "I wouldn't even compare it."

I told him, "I once burned my hand rather severely and experienced a pain unlike anything I have ever known before or since. Did you ever burn yourself?"

He said, "Yes, I knocked a can of gasoline off a shelf over a candle onto my leg and set my remaining leg on fire. As a result I spent several weeks in the hospital." He raised his pants leg and showed me the scars.

I said, "I know of nothing in this world that compares to the pain of burning. How did the pain you experienced when you died compare with that?"

He answered, "It was one thousand times worse than when my leg was on fire! I tried every way I knew to explain that away, but everything dissolved before my attempts to do it. I did not believe in hell before, and I did not want to believe in it then. On the face of this earth, no matter what you did to me, I don't think you could experience the pain that I experienced in that hospital."

I asked, "What do you think that was?"

"Why, I feel that it definitely had to be something other than on this earth, so the only place I can think of is that there must be a hell, and I was in it." He told me that when he thought about that after he got out of the hospital, he began to tremble with an uncontrollable trembling.

Hell is real! He believed it did not exist at all, just as some who are reading this believe. He thought it was a myth. He did not believe Christ. He did not believe God; he did not believe the Bible. But he died, and he believes it now! Tragically, some will only believe it when they experience it—when it will be too late.

If the Bible teaches anything at all, it is that there is an everlasting too late—that there will come a moment when it will be eternally too late, when the door of grace will have slammed shut forever. Then the sinner would give the universe itself for just one minute to repent and turn to Jesus Christ.

I believe there is a hell because Jesus Christ not only taught it, He also experienced it. We read in the Scripture that on the cross of Calvary, Christ took upon Himself the sin of the world; He was made sin for us, and our guilt was imputed to Him. God the Father looked down upon His beloved Son whom He had loved everlastingly, in whom He was well pleased, and saw Him as the Lamb of God that taketh away the sin of the world. And God poured out the caldron of His wrath against sin itself and it all poured out upon Jesus Christ who cried, "My God, my God, why hast thou forsaken me?" (Mathew 27:46), and then descended into hell.

In that darkness at noon Christ suffered an infinite penalty there upon the cross in our place. He said, "It is finished. It is paid." Those who will trust in Him can hear His words that the wages of sin, though it is death, is paid forever by Christ. And those who place their trust in Him have His word that they will never perish. The truth of the Scripture is that the anger and wrath of God will one day fall upon our sins. The only question is: Will it fall upon us in hell forever? Or will it fall upon Jesus Christ upon the cross? That choice is ours to make. We will live forever somewhere!

CHAPTER SEVEN

WHY I BELIEVE IN
MORAL ABSOLUTES

Woe unto them that call evil good, and good evil; that put darkness for light, and light for darkness; that put bitter for sweet, and sweet for bitter!

ISAIAH 5:20

Even the most cursory examination of the age in which we live will reveal an enormous decay and disintegration in the moral standards of the Western world. The evidence is everywhere. Many astute observers believe there is no hope for our civilization unless something is done about it.

The severance from life of moral ethics in the sense of any absolutes, as brought into our educational system by John Dewey and other naturalists, has brought a distressing situation to our world. In the very first sentence of the very first paragraph of the Introduction to his monumental book titled *The Closing of the American Mind*, Dr. Allan Bloom, Professor in the Committee on Social Thought at the University of Chicago, says this: "There is one thing a professor can be absolutely certain of. Almost every student entering the university believes, or says he believes, that truth is relative."

It's true. Virtually all our high school students have learned that there are no absolutes, that truth is relative. Mark Twain said that the problem with most people is not what they don't know but what they know for certain isn't true.

You probably heard about the teacher who said to his class, "You can know nothing for certain."

One student responded, "Teacher, are you sure?"

He said, "I'm certain."

To say there are no absolutes, however, is to say there is no God. God is the ultimate absolute, and what He says is the ultimate and absolute truth. And therein lies the moral quandary of the modern age. And it is getting worse as man sinks deeper into the mire of his own depravity.

Dr. Carl F. H. Henry, one of the keenest minds of our century, states: "Flares of distress signals emblazon the whole field of human behavior. Christianity's millennium-long barricade against a resurging paganism is weakening before the onslaughts of iniquity. Powerful forces aim to alter, discredit, even to replace it. As a result, the strength of Christian loyalties bulwark modern man's conduct less and less; moral earnestness almost everywhere halts indecisively at the Christian-pagan crossroads. In our decade, as many habitués of Sodom have detoured in the 'civilized' as into the 'uncivilized' half of the world."[1]

On a plane recently I was catching up on the news through an issue of *Newsweek*. The cover story focused on the moral situation in our country, especially the burgeoning flood of hard-core pornography. Over the years, many hun-

WHY I BELIEVE IN MORAL ABSOLUTES

dreds of people have come into my office to talk, and quite a few of them start by saying, "Now, I am probably going to shock you." I have always sort of smiled and thought that I had heard ten times worse than whatever they were going to tell me, that if anyone in the room would be shocked, it would not be me. I thought I was shockproof. But what I saw in this magazine shocked me!

Over the last several decades, moral standards in our country have sunk to alarming depths. Discussion of any sort of illicit sexual act was formerly considered shocking even between unmarried people; now adultery has become a commonplace subject for magazines, movies, and morning and afternoon TV serials. Homosexuality occupies the scene, but the more current obsession with bestiality threatens to usurp its place. The matter that I find truly shocking is the growing fad in hard-core pornographic magazines. Many deal with nothing but children between the ages of six and eleven, showing these little boys and girls in both heterosexual and homosexual acts. Moral paralysis seems to have gripped our nation!

Dr. Henry says that the present disintegration of Western culture represents a considerable inability to reconcile the competing demands of morality. In the current babble of voices, each asserting its own truth, the modern man is not convinced of the truth of any moral claim. Consequently, modern man seems unable to clearly formulate any sense of "ought." We are constantly exposed to various ethical and moral systems; unfortunately, few people clearly see these systems for what they are. Confused by them, they do not know how to respond to them.

Recently I heard a radio talk show in which a man was defending his homosexuality. In so doing, he was setting forth a whole moral ethical system. I wondered how many people listening to him had any grasp of the basic ethical foundations upon which he was operating or the fallacies of that system. He presented such a convincing case that the host of the show seemed unable to cope with it.

We should keep in mind that every television program, every newscast, every magazine, every novel, every motion picture is based on some ethical presupposition, derived from among a wide variety of ethical systems. Unfortunately (and this is irritating to me), many Christians just do not want to bother their heads to learn about them; consequently, they are totally incapable of dealing with this wave of immorality based on spurious ethical foundations that is inundating our country. Everything that we do is based upon some ethical, moral consideration, and I am afraid that most of us operate only under the fuzziest concepts of what we really are about.

Let us take a look at the whole matter of ethics. It is important to know, first of all, that there are two great divisions in ethical systems. One ethical system is based upon revelation, an ethical system God has revealed in the Scriptures of the Old and New Testaments. It is God given; in the words of theology, it is theonomous, a God-law. "Thy Word is truth," says John 17:17. In Matthew 5:18, Christ said, "Till heaven and earth pass away, one jot or one tittle shall in no wise pass from the law till all be fulfilled." The Bible declares that is the truth revealed from God, and therefore absolutely true. The other main division, called speculative ethics, is an entirely different system, one that is invented by man. It is humanistic and autonomous in its nature. It comes from below upward, whereas the other comes from above.

People will say that things are always changing, and that is certainly true. What was true ten years ago may not be true today. That is true in the mores of people, but it is not true with God or with revelational ethics. God is immutable, unchangeable, and His truth changes not. It doesn't matter if everyone in the world joins hands and votes unanimously that God's truth is false, it still remains true. It remains true whether I believe in it or I don't believe in it. Whether you accept or reject it does not alter the fact that God's truth does exist and never changes.

Most college students will, during the course of their studies in philosophy, enter into that branch of philosophy known as ethics. In most cases, they will find that revelational ethics is totally ignored and speculative human ethics occupies the entire field of endeavor.

Let us look at the ethical systems upon which the unregenerate world and, unfortunately, too many Christians unknowingly operate.

In the speculative realm of ethics, there are two broad divisions. First of all, there is naturalism, which begins with the premise that man is totally matter. He is a complex animal, and his well-being involves something of an adjustment to the physical universe in which he exists. All sorts of ethical systems spring out of this concept.

The other great division is idealism. This begins from a totally opposite premise: that there is a basic immaterial reality, a spiritual reality, a mental reality, a rational reality, if you will, that is primary, preexistent to matter and of much more importance than matter. From this idealistic base, a number of rationalistic systems have evolved, such as those held by Plato, Socrates, and others, as well as all of the pantheistic systems.

Out of these two major divisions spring a number of different systems of ethics. One is pragmatism, which operates upon the principle that if something works, then it is good. Obviously, this system has no moral foundation. Hitler was succeeding pretty well in destroying all the Jews in Europe.

When that system was working fairly well, its apparent success would have been a guarantee that it was morally good. A bank robber may be successful but that does not prove that bank robbing is good. A businessman may be tremendously successful in his business, but the fact of his success does not mean that what he is doing is good.

Another system is egoism, from the word *ego*, which means: "I will seek that which is good for me." The system of altruism says: "What we must seek is the good of others." So, we find individualism based upon egoism. Communism and socialism, among others, are based upon the idea that man's good is for the state, and their concern is for society rather than the individual. Numerous other systems stem from these basic foundations. All of these systems contain certain conflicts or antitheses, opposite polarities with which they struggle. All these systems are alike in that they are incomplete and inadequate. None of them are as well-rounded as the scriptural system, which covers all of the basic needs of mankind and society.

Many systems contain conflicts between the religious and the ethical. There have been various religious approaches to life that have ignored the ethical aspects of life and have concentrated simply upon spiritual things. There have been, on the other hand, those who have emphasized simply the ethical aspects of life and have ignored the religious. Both of these believed that they had some sort of ethical system, but each was only partial.

It is unfortunate that so many people are operating under unclear, unsophisticated ethical systems they have never critically analyzed. Most of these turn out to be poor images of some pagan system or little parts of some larger part of the Christian system. To compound the confusion, there seems to be a mistaken idea that just because a "system" is simple enough that it has been grasped, it automatically carries the divine imprimatur.

I have known many people who think that if they just try to keep the second table of the law, which deals with man's relationship to his fellowman, they can ignore the first table, which deals with man's relationship to God, or vice versa. I have known others who suppose because they have been honest and have been faithful to their wives and kind to their neighbors, that in some way, they are right with God. Unfortunately, they have a cafeteria-style morality, picking and choosing those commandments they prefer to try to keep and ignoring the rest.

Perhaps you know someone whose ethical system goes something like this: "My rule for living is 'I would never intentionally hurt anyone else.'" Or you may have heard someone say: "Well, I have never really hurt anyone, so I'm sure I'm going to be all right with God." How utterly foolish! The first statement carries no intent to include God. The second altogether ignores the fact that we are to worship God—to learn about Him—to serve Him. The person who has done none of these things has omitted the most important part of God's law.

Numerous ethical systems have stressed the libertarian concepts of man's free will; that is, that all of our ethical decisions are based on man's free will. On the other hand, there have been those who have emphasized determinism and necessity, stating that man is not free but is controlled by some outside force. Fatalism says that impersonal fates control our lives. You say, "Well, that's pretty ancient. Do people really believe that?" Yes. And there are millions of them in America, consulting the astrological tables because they are convinced that some force in the heavens is controlling their lives, just as the moon controls the tides.

The most popular form of psychology today, behavioristic psychology, is completely deterministic. Man is determined by what he eats, by all things that impinge upon him; not merely his physical body but his ideas and his morality are determined by his environment. Therefore, changing his environment will change the man. This deterministic system is so prevalent that it controls much of the thinking in our society today. Most people do not even realize what kind of system they are dealing with or why people argue as they do; for example, that all we need to do is clean up a slum in order to change people for the better. Recent studies have shown that the environment of a person is by no means the crucial factor in the type of life he or she lives.

Then there is the conflict between teleological and ateleological ethical systems. Both words are derived from the Greek word *telos* meaning "the end." *Teleological* pertains to the study of the end—the end result. The prefix *a* in *ateleological* means "away from," thus the word has the meaning of not considering the end. Some systems say the most important determining factor in ethics is: What will be the end result of my action? People who adopt this view act as though the only consideration in an action's being moral or immoral is what its end is going to be. This provides the basis for utilitarianism, which says: Our goal must be the greatest good of the greatest number, and it is the end that will determine whether something is good or not.

That may sound quite plausible, but there is a problem: How do we compute whether the end is good or not? For example, you decide that you are going to give someone a book. Do you know what the end result will be? A very devout Christian gave to a young graduate in theology the book *The Principles of Geology* by Lyell. The man to whom he gave it was Charles Darwin. The result: control of the universities of the world by evolutionary thought. It all began when someone gave a book to a man who was about to set sail on a worldwide voyage. None of us can compute what the results of our actions might be. When we do something to our children, we don't know what might happen three or four generations in the future because of that action. This is why teleological ethics always fail. A couple of examples of teleological ethics are socialism and communism.

A form of the egoistic ethic says: The important thing is

simply for me to consider whether a certain action will bring pleasure to me. Hedonism is the name for this idea that the goal in life is pleasure. An egoistic hedonism is the idea that I must seek something that will bring me pleasure. When you eat a piece of pie à la mode, will that bring you pleasure or pain? You contemplate committing adultery with someone—is that going to bring you pleasure or pain? What will happen down through the generations? Every action has eternal ramifications; therefore, it is impossible that anyone could ever establish a moral principle based on teleological ethics.

Ateleological ethics stress not the end but the beginning—the motive. The only matter of importance is that the motive must be right. Many times we hear, "If anyone is sincere, then it must be right. It doesn't matter what religion one embraces, as long as one is sincere." Well, the mother was perfectly sincere at 3:00 A.M. when she gave her child that cough medicine; however, the next morning she noticed that it was Mercurochrome and the child was dead. She was sincere, but people can be sincerely wrong.

The entire basis of that prevalent modern ethical system, the "New Morality" or situational ethics, is: The only thing that matters is our motive, which must be love. That sounds plausible, doesn't it? Then one reads some of the cases set forth in their books. For example: Here is a poor young lady. She has no boyfriends, and she is all tied up emotionally. Now, if you would just have an affair with this young lady, you would probably set her free and release all of her inhibitions and start her on a new life. So, under the motive of love, you break one of the commandments of God. We can see that both ateleological and teleological ethics, in themselves, always fail.

With relativistic morals also comes subjectivism. We no longer talk about morals, we talk about "values"—a term that Nietzsche gave to us. Values are simply anything that anyone chooses to place a value upon. Somehow, we have come to a place of believing that every person has some authority to decide what is good or bad for him or her, what is of value and what is not of value.

Of course, a corollary of that is that a person cannot impose his or her values upon anyone else. That is absolutely true, as long as we are talking about merely values, which we have simply accepted. God's law, however, applies to all created beings, because He is the Creator and He applies it to all without exception.

Another corollary is that since our values and mores do not come from God, they must come from some source that influences us, and that source is cultural. So these values, these morals, are relativistic, individual, subjective, and culturally induced. This view was taught and accepted on a university level around the world for most of the first half of our century. However, society found out that when taken to its limits, cultural relativism is not tolerable, either.

During the Nuremberg War Trials after World War II, Nazi leaders were brought before that court and charged with all manner of crimes, including the slaughtering of millions of Jews and other people. What was their defense? It was a clever one. The Supreme Court in Germany had declared that Jews were nonpersons. So these indicted Nazi leaders said, "We have done nothing wrong. We acted according to our own culture, according to our own mores, according to our own laws. We were told that they could be killed. Who are you to come from another culture, another society, and impose your morals on us?"

The Allied attorneys were thrown for a fifty-yard loss. They didn't know what to say. If there are no absolutes, if everything is relativistic, if everything is culturally induced and we have no authority to impose our culture upon another, how dare we say that the Nazis were wrong for killing millions of people. The lawyers were so taken aback, that after huddling for some time, they finally decided to retreat. Since they apparently were not willing to retreat to the moral law of God, they retreated to "natural law," which has been held through many centuries. Although it is less precise, more vague, it nevertheless still has some moral content to it. The lawyers appealed to natural laws, and it was on that basis that the Nazis were convicted.

Having made this brief summary of some of the ethical systems prevalent today, I would like to caution you to remember three things about each of these systems. First, all of the speculative systems are just that; they are speculations. They are rationalistic. They reject revelation and base the whole weight of their support simply upon the conceptions of the human mind. Therefore, their limitations should be obvious at once. We don't live our lives relativistically because we live in an "absolute" world. Suppose you are waiting in your car at a train crossing and a train is coming down the tracks at sixty miles an hour. You know that if you drive your car out in front of that train, you are not going to be "relatively" dead. You are going to be "absolutely" dead. So as we try to live by such thinking, we continue to be confused.

Second, the systems are all man-centered, and man becomes his own god. In every one of these systems, it is man who will decide what he is going to do. Thus God is banished from his universe, and the Creator has no right to tell the creature what to do. Man has become a law unto himself, the autonomous man.

Third, all human ethical systems are a willful rebellion against the Almighty God. They attempt to allow man to live a life not controlled by God and His law, but still justify himself as an ethical and moral being. In the Scriptures we have an ethical system that is perfectly balanced and that will meet all the needs of the human heart. First of all, it deals with man's motive. Having come to Jesus Christ and found forgiveness, man is released from the burden and bondage of guilt and fear. He is allowed to serve God in gratitude and love. Paul said, "The love of Christ constraineth us" (2 Corinthians 5:14). The gratitude of the heart causes those who have been redeemed and have received the free gift of eternal life to want to live for God; therefore, the motive is made right.

Not only is the motive right, but the end is right. In the Hebrew-Christian tradition, it is obviously clear that the good is inevitably connected with God, who is the ultimate good and the giver of every good and perfect gift. All human systems try to find man's good apart from God, and thus they fall to the ground. Our highest good is to know God, to be like Him, to love Him, to glorify Him, to enjoy Him forever!

The ethical system in the Scriptures not only gives the proper motive and proper end, but it also provides an easily applicable instruction for our daily life in the law God has given to us. This law is to be obeyed not out of a servile fear, as a slave obeys a master, but out of a heart of filial love, as a child obeys a beloved parent.

The law God has given us does several things. The first purpose we should clearly see is that it sets before us a standard of what God would have us to be; a perfect standard of what our lives should be like. We don't have to grope in the darkness to know whether something is right or wrong.

Second, and this is often missed, the law is given to convince us that we fail to keep it. By the law is the knowledge of sin. The law convicts. Martin Luther called the law a mirror; as we look into the mirror of God's law we see all of our wrinkles and moles and other disfigurations—all of our guilt, sin, and uncleanness. Luther also called the law a hammer—a hammer that smashes our self-righteousness.

When a person makes up his own ethical code, he always makes up an ethical system he thinks he has kept. In the law of God, we find a law that smashes our self-righteousness, eliminates all trust in our own goodness, and convinces us that we are sinners. The law of God leaves us with our hands over our mouths and our faces in the dust. We are humbled before God and convinced that we are guilty transgressors of His law. Luther said, "The law is a whip that drives us to the cross." But God does not leave us in our uncleanness, nor does He leave us in our abased state of guilt and corruption. He drives us to the cross—the source of grace—so that we may look up into the face of Jesus

Christ. There we find the One who will cleanse us, the One who will remove all of our guilt, the One who can empower us by His spirit to endeavor to keep His law henceforth. This is the purpose of God's law.

How may we meet this standard, which is perfection? Jesus said, "Be ye therefore perfect, even as your Father which is in heaven is perfect" (Matthew 5:48). God's ethical system is one that demands perfection. Unless we have perfect ethical, moral records, we will never get into heaven. If we offend in one point, we are guilty of all—in one thought, in one word, in one deed, or in one omission or one commission. God is of purer eyes than even to look upon iniquity, and *no sin* will ever enter heaven. How, then, can we ever hope to live up to this perfect standard that God has given? The answer is: *we can't* but *God did*. The way of man is to pull God's standard down to the place where man can get over it. God's way was to lower Himself to the cross and into hell itself in order to pay for our sins—that He might lift us up to His perfect standard.

Everyone in the world seems to be trusting basically in the obedience of one of two people. If we were to ask ourselves, "What is my hope of eternal life?" we might answer: "I have never hurt anyone. I have tried to follow the Golden Rule. I have tried to keep the commandments. I have gone to church. I have prayed. I have given money to the poor. I have been kind to my neighbor." If so, we are trusting in our own righteousness to get us to heaven. The problem is: "There is none righteous, no, not one" (Romans 3:10). "All our righteousnesses are as filthy rags" (Isaiah 64:6); sin taints every day of our lives. Therefore, as long as we trust in ourselves, we will *never* make it. We need to trust in the obedience of another person—*Jesus Christ*—the *only* One who ever lived according to the perfect standard of God; the only One who never sinned; that one who is without blemish, who was tempted in all ways, as we are, yet without sin.

The Bible says that the perfect life of Jesus Christ was not only lived as an *example* for us (which many people grasp), but it was also lived *substitutionarily*. Christ lived His perfect life in our place, and He is willing to clothe us with His obedience, that we may stand faultless before God, clothed in the righteousness of Jesus Christ. One of the names of Jehovah in the Old Testament is, "The Lord our Righteousness" (Jeremiah 23:6). Christ is our righteousness. His life was lived in our place. The Scripture says, "By the obedience of one shall many be made righteous" (Romans 5:19).

We will come before God either clothed in our own righteousness (when the lights go on, we will see that we are clothed in filthy rags), or we will come clothed in the righteousness of Jesus Christ, the only perfect One. In whose goodness shall we trust? Our own? Or Christ's?

I am astounded to learn how many people sit in church year after year and suppose that all Christianity says to people is: "Be good; try harder." They fail totally to understand even the most basic, elementary message of Christianity that in ourselves we have no hope; that our righteousness in which so many trust is simply filthy rags. Paul described it as "dung" (Philippians 3:8).

We are to be found in Christ by faith in Him. By trusting in what He did, we may be clothed in His righteousness and thus stand faultless before the Throne of God. This is the glorious Good News—the message of the gospel—though you and I are sinners—unclean, undeserving, ill-deserving, hell-deserving—Christ, the All-Deserving One, lived and died in our stead. If we trust in Him, we will get not what we deserve, but what He deserves—paradise.

CHAPTER EIGHT

WHY I BELIEVE IN CHRIST

For in him dwelleth all the fulness of the Godhead bodily.

COLOSSIANS 2:9

Why do people believe in Christ? Is it because of some emotion, some peculiar predisposition, some desire to believe with one's heart what one knows with one's mind not to be true? Is there any real evidence?

Christianity is the only religion in the world that is based upon historic evidences. The Bible never calls us to blind faith but always to a faith in those things that have been established by evidence. The evidence for Jesus Christ is absolutely overwhelming. No one can disbelieve in Christ because of a lack of evidence.

Let us consider some of the reasons why we believe in Jesus Christ. In this great debate of the centuries, Johann Wolfgang Goethe, perhaps the most sophisticated of the

German poets and literati, said, "The conflict of faith and unbelief remains the proper, the only, the deepest theme of the history of the world and mankind, to which all others are subordinated." The great issue that this world struggle is all about is whether or not we believe in Jesus Christ. Dr. Philip Schaff, an eminent historian and professor at Yale University, cautions us with this warning: "Infidels are seldom convinced by argument; for the springs of unbelief are in the heart rather than in the head."[1] A reprobate mind and heart bring forth ungodly words, deeds, and actions.

Another Christian and I were in the midst of a number of ungodly men from whose mouths flowed forth a constant effusion of filth, and as we moved away, my friend said, "The reprobate mind—at enmity with God." How true it is! Dr. Schaff continues, "But honest inquirers and earnest skeptics, like Nathanael and Thomas, who love the truth, and wish only for tangible support of their weak faith, will never refuse, when the evidence is laid before them, to embrace it with grateful joy, and to worship the incarnate God."[2] For those who are honest seekers after the truth there is abundant evidence.

Jesus Christ—what shall we say about Him? He is the founder of the largest religion in the history of the world. Christianity is twice as large as its closest competitor. Today there are one billion three hundred and twenty million people who claim to be Christians.

What shall we say about Jesus? Some have said He was just a myth; He never really existed. This is one possibility that we might consider.

One historian has written that the wisest opponents of Christianity have abandoned the legendary hypothesis as utterly incompatible. Historian J. Gilchrist Lawson says: "The legendary, or mythical, theory of Christ's existence is not held by any one worthy of the name of scholar. The historical evidences of Christ's existence are so much greater than those in support of any other event in ancient history; no candid scholar could reject them without also renouncing his belief in every event recorded in ancient history."[3] The evidence for the historicity of Christ is so great I know of no historian in the free world who would dare place his or her reputation on the chopping block by denying that Jesus Christ ever existed.

How do we know that He existed? Is it simply because the Bible tells us so? That *is* one reason. We have four biographies of Christ in the Scripture, and the testimony of the Gospel historians is far more accurate and detailed than that of any secular historian, as we have already discussed in earlier chapters.

Some people suppose that, other than the Gospels, no ancient writer mentions Jesus Christ. They are quite wrong. Among the secular historians and writers of antiquity who refer to Christ and Christianity are: Tacitus, the Roman historian; Suetonius; Pliny the younger; Epictetus; Lucian; Aristides; Galenus; Lampridius; DioCassius; Hinnerius; Libanius; Ammianus; Marcellinus; Eunapius; Zosimus. Others have written whole books against Christianity, including Lucian, Celsus, Porphyry, Hierocles, and Julian the Apostate. Numerous others, including Jewish writers, have written about Jesus Christ.

So abundant is the testimony to Christ that Dr. Philip Schaff says: "Standing on this rock, I feel safe against all the attacks of infidelity. The person of Christ is to me the greatest and surest of all facts; as certain as my own personal existence."[4]

Pontius Pilate, procurator of Judea who condemned Christ to death, wrote of those extraordinary activities to Tiberius Caesar in an apparently well-known account that has been referred to by several other historic personages. One Christian apologist, some years later, writing to another Caesar, encouraged him to check with his own archives and discover from the report of Pontius Pilate that these things were true. In this long report, after describing the miracles of Christ, Pilate states: "And him Herod and Archelaus and Philip, Annas and Caiaphas, with all the people, delivered to me, making a great uproar against me that I should try him [Christ]. I therefore ordered him to be crucified, having first scourged him, and having found against him no cause of evil accusations or deeds. And at the time he was crucified there was darkness over all the world, the sun being darkened at mid-day, and the stars appearing, but in them there appeared no lustre; and the moon, as if turned into blood, failed in her light."[5]

Another secular writer, Thallus, in A.D. 52, writes about the sun's failure to give light from noon until three o'clock and says that this must have been due to an eclipse. However, we know that Christ was crucified at the time of the Passover, which was the time of the full moon, and there cannot be an eclipse of the sun at the time of the full moon.[6] Yet this writer felt he must offer some naturalistic explanation for the phenomenon of the sun's ceasing to give its light.

F. F. Bruce, Rylands professor of biblical criticism and exegesis at the University of Manchester, says: "Some writers may toy with the fancy of a 'Christ-myth,' but they do not do so on the ground of historical evidence. The historicity of Christ is as axiomatic for an unbiased historian as the historicity of Julius Caesar. It is not historians who propagate the 'Christ-myth' theories."[7] Tacitus, discussing Nero's attempt to cover up his burning of Rome, wrote this: "Hence to suppress the rumor, he falsely charged with the guilt, and punished with the most exquisite tortures, the persons commonly called Christians, who were hated for their enormities. Christus, the founder of the name, was put to death by Pontius Pilate, procurator of Judea in the reign of Tiberius; but the pernicious superstition, repressed for a time, broke out again, not only through Judea, where the mischief originated, but through the city of Rome also."[8] So Tacitus reminds us that Christ was crucified by Pontius Pilate during the reign of Tiberius Caesar. He reminds us also that it was Christ—Christus—who was the founder of the Christian religion, which had spread throughout Judea and all the way to Rome by this time. Pliny the younger, who was putting Christians to death—men and women and boys and girls—finally wrote the emperor, Trajan, seeking counsel. He wondered if he should kill all Christians or just certain ones. In the same letter he says: "They affirmed, however, that the whole of their guilt, or their error, was that they were in the habit of meeting on a certain fixed day before it was light, when they sang in alternate verse a hymn to Christ as to a god, and bound themselves to a solemn oath, not to do any wicked deeds."[9] So we find from Pliny that the Christians believed that Jesus Christ was God, and they met early one day each week and worshiped Him.

An early Syrian writer, Mara Bar-Scrapion, in about A.D. 73, wrote to his son warning him not to get involved in wicked deeds and reminding him of the terrible consequences that came upon people for killing godly men. He also stated, "What advantage did the Jews gain from executing their wise King? It was just after that that their kingdom was abolished. God justly avenged these wise men. . . . The Jews, ruined and driven from their land, live in complete dispersion."[10] But the teachings of their wise King live on.

Julian the Apostate endeavored to destroy Christianity. He wrote a whole book against it, but in that book, instead of destroying Christianity, he *affirms* that Jesus was born in the reign of Augustus at the time of the taxing made in Judea by Cyrenius. He also confirms the fact that the Christian religion began its rise in the times of the emperors Tiberius and Claudius. He affirms the authenticity of the Gospels of Matthew, Mark, Luke, and John as the authentic sources of the Christian religion. This same Julian went to Jerusalem to disprove the Bible, but he failed. When, unknowingly, he destroyed the wall of Babylon, he confirmed the biblical prophecy. When he finally came to his death, pointing his dagger up to the sky at Jesus, he gathered his blood after being wounded on the battlefield, threw it into the air, and said, "Thou has conquered, O Galilean."[11] Julian left behind no trace of the paganism he endeavored to rebuild. All of his efforts evaporated before the power of the Galilean.

Many other writers have spoken of Christ. Josephus, the famous Jewish historian, tells us that there arose at this time a great man, whom the leaders of his people had put to death by Pontius Pilate, and this was the Christ.[12]

There have been those who say this is an interpolation, that Josephus would never have said that Jesus was the Christ, and never said that "our leaders committed a wicked deed by putting him to death." Josephus turned coat and surrendered to the Romans and lived in Rome under the benefits of the caesar. And who can say whether or not he ever truly accepted Christ? Those who try to get rid of the passage have only their prejudices to back them up because every single manuscript of the writings of Josephus contains within it that passage as well as mentions of James, a brother of Jesus, and John the Baptist and other things found in the New Testament. So we see that the historicity of Jesus Christ is something that cannot be assailed; it is not a myth or a legend!

Add these historic records to the canon of ancient books we call the Bible, and its fulfilled prophecies about Christ only add more proof. There are 333 prophecies in the Old Testament that deal with the promised Messiah, and of those 333 texts, 456 specific details of His life and coming are indeed delineated for us. One of the purposes for God's giving the Old Testament to the Jewish people was to be able to identify the Messiah when He came from among them. Prophecies are usually vague by nature; not the ones in the Word of God.

The Messianic prophecies of Scripture are amazingly clear. Listen to only a few of them: that the seed of the woman—a reference to the Virgin Birth since there is no other such reference in all of the Bible—would destroy the seed of the serpent, Satan. That He would come from the line of Abraham. That He would be from the house of David. That He would be called Immanuel. That He would have a forerunner who would proclaim His coming. That He would be born in Bethlehem Ephratah of Judea *not* Bethlehem Zebulen of Israel. That He would be worshiped by wise men giving gifts. That Bethlehem would suffer a massacre of infants upon the king's hearing of Jesus' birth. That He would be called a Nazarene.

The list could go on and on—456 specific details from the prophecies. Stop and think. One might be a weak argument for Christ. But 456? It's like walking down a road by the edge of a cliff and having a rock fall off. You could easily step around one rock, but if there's an avalanche of rocks, you would not be able to escape its impact.

What about the unique character of this One that we *know* existed? Through studying many biographies, I have found something that all historians have discovered—the more you look at any human being, the more the luster grows dim. No matter how great the hero may have been, if you examine him closely, you see his feet of clay; you see all his frailties and foibles. Dr. Schaff says that all human greatness diminishes on closer inspection; but Christ's character grows more pure, sacred, and lovely the better we know Him.

The whole range of history and fiction furnishes no parallel to it. There never has been anyone like Jesus Christ. The more His life is studied, the more impressive it is. Only those people who are ignorant of His life could ever say anything to deprecate it. When His life is examined, He is seen as the altogether lovely One; He is the incomparable Christ; He is the Crystal Christ. As Sidney Lanier said, "What is there in him that we would find to forgive? He is the One who never did anything amiss; the only One with whom no one has ever been able to find any fault; the One who could say, 'Which of you convinceth me of sin?'" He is the perfect man, the perfect example of humanity.

Sometimes people say, "Only ignorant people would believe that Christ was a great person." Listen to some of the most brilliant minds that have ever lived. Jean Jacques Rousseau, one of the great intellects of France and a great opponent of Christianity, later in his life admitted in his *Emile* that there could be no comparison between Socrates and Christ; as little as between a sage and God. Goethe, that sophisticated genius of Germany, said of Jesus that He was "the Divine Man," "the Holy One." Jean Paul Friedrich Richter said, "He is the purest among the mighty, the mightiest among the pure." Ernest Renan, the great orientalist, linguist, French scholar, and critic, who tried to tear the Bible to pieces, after all his attempts later called Christ "a man of colossal dimensions"; "the incomparable man, to whom the universal conscience has decreed the title of *Son of God*, and that with justice, since he caused religion to take a step in advance incomparably greater than any other in the past, and probably any yet to come." Renan closes his *Life of Jesus* with the remarkable concession: "Whatever may be the surprises of the future, *Jesus will never be surpassed*."[13] Rousseau also said, "Shall we suppose the evangelical history a mere fiction? Indeed it bears no marks of fiction. . . . On the contrary, the history of Socrates, which no one presumes to doubt, is not so well attested as that of Jesus Christ."[14]

You have often heard the famous testimony Napoleon Bonaparte gave on the island of St. Helena: "I know men; and I tell you that Jesus Christ is not a man." After an ungodly life

Napoleon came to his end there on that barren island. Reading the Scripture each day, he came to these conclusions: "Superficial minds see a resemblance between Christ and the founders of empires, and the gods of other religions. That resemblance does not exist. There is between Christianity and whatever other religions the distance of infinity. We can say to the authors of every other religion, 'You are neither gods nor the agents of the Deity. You are but missionaries of false-hood, molded from the same clay with the rest of mortals. You are made with all the passions and vices inseparable from them. Your temples and your priests proclaim your origin.' Such will be the judgment, the cry of conscience, of whoever examines the gods and the temples of paganism." But Jesus Christ, he said, astounded him and filled him with awe.[15]

William Shakespeare, perhaps the greatest literary genius of all time, wrote in his will: "I commend my soul into the hands of God, my Creator, hoping and assuredly believing, through the merits of Jesus Christ my Savior to be made par-taker of Life everlasting." Lord Byron: "If ever man was God or God man, Jesus Christ was both." James Greenleaf Whittier: "My ground of hope for myself and for humanity is in that divine fullness of love which was manifested in the life, teaching, and sacrifice of Christ. In the infinite mercy of God so revealed and not in any worth or merit of our nature, I humbly, yet very hopefully trust." Charles Dickens: "I com-mit my soul to the mercy of God, through our Lord and Savior Jesus Christ. I now most solemnly impress upon you the truth and beauty of the Christian religion as it came from Christ himself, and the impossibility of going far wrong if you humbly but heartily respect it." Leo Tolstoi, the great genius of Russian letters who once was an atheist of the wildest sort, said this: "For thirty-five years of my life I was, in the proper acceptation of the word a nihilist—not a revolutionary socialist, but a man who believed in nothing. Five years ago my faith came to me. I believed in the doctrine of Jesus, and my whole life underwent a sudden transformation. . . . Life and death ceased to be evil; instead of despair I tasted joy and happiness that death could not take away."[16]

Goethe said: "I look upon all four Gospels as thoroughly genuine, for there shines forth from them the reflected splendor of a sublimity proceeding from Jesus Christ." George Bancroft, the great American historian, says that he sees the name of Jesus Christ written across every page of modern history. William E. H. Lecky, a great skeptic and unbeliever, author of *The History of Rationalism in Europe*, analyzed the whole history of thought through all of the ages of Europe. He said: "It was reserved for Christianity to present to the world an Ideal Character, which through all the changes of eighteen centuries, has filled the hearts of man with an impassioned love, and has shown itself capable of acting on all ages, nations, temperaments, conditions; and which has not only been the highest pattern of virtue, but the highest incentive to its practice." Ruskin, Lessing, Webster, Wagner, and innumerable others agreed.[17]

There are books filled with thousands of testimonies of the greatest minds this world has ever produced. Jesus Christ was, Himself, the greatest person this world has ever known. Simply from the writings of those who totally disbelieved in Christianity, you can attest the fact that Christ is the greatest human who ever lived in this world. Pilate called Him "the man without fault." Diderot called Him "the unsurpassed." Napoleon called Him "the emperor of Love." David Friedrich Strauss, that great German critic, called Him "the highest model of religion." John Stuart Mill, whose writings have led some to say he was the most intelligent man who ever lived, called Christ "the guide of humanity." Lecky called Him "the highest pattern of virtue." Pecant called Him "the Holy One before God." Martineau called Him "the divine flower of humanity." Renan called Him "the greatest among the sons of men." Theodore Parker called Him "the youth with God in his heart." Francis Cobb called Him "the regenerator of humanity." Robert Owen called Him "the irreproachable."[18]

None of these things will do. Jesus Christ is infinitely more than all of that! He is the Divine Creator of the universe, the One without whom nothing was made that has been made; who came into this world to die for the human creature's sin. He is God incarnate! He is the One who declared that "before Abraham was, I am" (John 8:58); the One who said: "My Father worketh hitherto, and I work" (John 5:17); the One who said, "I and my Father are one" (John 10:30). He demands absolute submission to His will. He demands to be Lord and Master and King of our lives. He demands that we repent of our sins and that we bring every thought into captivity unto Him; that we wholly and completely surrender to His Lordship and His Saviorhood.

Jesus Christ is real, and one day we will know that for a fact because before Him every knee shall bow. All who have ever lived—the most voluble atheist, the most rationalistic skeptic, the most wicked and profane and vile, will one day bow their knees and proclaim that He is the Lord of all!

All of these are reasons why I believe in Jesus Christ. But that is not how I first came to know Him. I first came to know Him when I saw Him lifted up before my eyes as the Divine Savior who loved me and was dying for my sins—this One whose brow was pierced; whose hands were skewered to a cross; this One who said, "Come unto me . . . and I will give you rest" (Matthew 11:28). I saw there the lover of my soul, that One who loved me more than father or mother or wife or child, that One who will love me everlastingly—the only One who even went to hell for me. I remember slipping off my chair onto my knees and inviting Him into my life. Why? Because I was moved by the Spirit of God and irresistibly drawn to Him. And thus I came to know and to believe in the living Christ, *my* Divine Redeemer.

CHAPTER NINE

WHY I BELIEVE IN THE VIRGIN BIRTH

And the angel answered and said unto her, The Holy Ghost shall come upon thee, and the power of the Highest shall overshadow thee: therefore also that holy thing which shall be born of thee shall be called the Son of God.

LUKE 1:35

I want to assure you right off that I do not believe in the Virgin Birth and hope that none of you do. Did that get your attention?

Those are not my words. Those are the words spoken from the magnificent Riverside Church in New York City more than a half century ago by the Reverend Harry Emerson Fosdick, leader and popularizer of the liberal theological movement in America.

For some reason, the Virgin Birth of Christ has come under greater attack than any other miracle in the New Testament. Not too long ago, a group calling themselves the Jesus Seminar grabbed headlines. The group consisted of a few dozen of the most liberal radical Bible theologians in America. Their purpose was to vote, using colored pebbles, on their opinion of the truth of the Gospel stories. This pebble-based research of theirs is really no research at all. It is merely an expression of their unbelief. They voted, for instance, that the Virgin Birth of Christ never occurred, that the visit of the wise men was fiction, and that the flight into Egypt was a flight of fancy.

However, I believe that the Virgin Birth is not only a fact but also a foundational fact of our faith.

The more deceptive kind of skeptics will not so much attack the Virgin Birth's truth directly, but suggest that it really doesn't matter. One day, I sat down to consider what difference it does make whether the Virgin Birth happened, and here are the differences I discovered:

1. If Jesus were not born of a virgin, then the New Testament narratives are proved false and unreliable.

2. Mary is stained with the sin of unchastity. She was, of course, betrothed to Joseph, which is more than our "engagement." To end a betrothal required a bill of divorcement, and if one of the two was unfaithful, the sin was not fornication but adultery. Unchastity in a woman meant she would be taken to the gate of the city, her clothes ripped, her jewelry removed, and then she would be dressed in rags, tied with a rope, and put on exhibit for all the other women of the city who would be brought out to gape at her as a warning for their own chastity. (Today, such unchastity gets you an invitation to a TV talk show.)

3. Jesus was mistaken about His paternity because He repeatedly declared that He was the Son of God, and that God was His Father.

4. Christ was not born of the "seed of the woman"; therefore, the ancient promise given in the Garden of Eden that the seed of the woman would destroy the head of the serpent is unfulfilled.

5. Jesus was, therefore, an illegitimate child, not the peerless Son of God.

6. He is consequently not the God-man.

7. He was then a sinner just like the rest of us.

8. As a sinner, He cannot be the Divine Redeemer, because the sacrifice must be perfect.

9. Therefore, we have no Savior at all.

10. We are yet in our sins and without forgiveness.

11. We have no hope after death.

12. There is no mediator between God and man.

13. There is no Trinity, because there is no Second Person of the Trinity.

14. Christ should not have prayed, "Father, forgive them" but rather, "Father, forgive us," because He was a sinner just like the rest of us.

15. Last, if this miracle of the Virgin Birth is denied, where shall we draw the line? Why should we not deny them all?

Does it make a difference? It makes all the difference in this world and in the world to come. If the Virgin Birth of

Christ is not true, it totally subverts the entire Christian gospel, destroys the whole meaning of Jesus Christ as a Divine Redeemer, and robs us of all hope of salvation.

Why, then, do some people not believe it if it is so important? Basically, there are three reasons. First, some deny the Virgin Birth because they deny miracles. They have an anti-supernatural bias. They would say that the only reason people believed in a virgin birth back then, was that the ancient people were ignorant of the scientific method and the natural laws, so they believed all sorts of things were miracles that were not really miracles.

True, Joseph was not as acquainted with childbirth and conception as the average gynecologist today. But Joseph was not a naive man. When he discovered that Mary was "with child," what did he do? Did he say, "Oh, it's probably a virgin birth. It's no doubt the Holy Spirit who has done this thing. Being such an ignorant old fool, I certainly don't believe that she slept with anyone else." No, instead, he determined to put her away privately, having concluded that she had been unchaste. It took a visitation from the Angel Gabriel to convince him of the concept of a virgin birth.

Dr. Manford George Gutzke, one of my seminary professors, used to say that the Virgin Birth is no big problem at all for God. If there is a God who created the universe, if He flung the galaxies out from His fingertips, if He painted the night sky with a scintillating Milky Way, then surely for Him to take a tiny seed and place it in the womb of a woman is nothing at all.

Keep in mind that when God created the world, we ar told

in Genesis 1 that He placed that same kind of seed in every animal, in every fruit, in every tree, in every plant that exists on this planet—billions and trillions of them. Why should it be thought impossible that God should simply place a "Y" chromosome in the womb of a woman to produce a child?

As Dr. Gutzke added, if you can't believe that God can do that little thing, you really don't believe in God at all. If He can't do that, He can't do much of anything.

Second, some people reject the Virgin Birth because, although they believe in some miracles, in the case of the Virgin Birth they claim that many other books in the Scriptures are silent about it. This is an argument called "the argument from silence."

The late Dr. Harry Rimmer, a well-educated Presbyterian minister, once had quite an encounter on the floor of a certain Presbytery with a rather radical minister in that Presbytery. A young man was being examined who had proclaimed that he did not believe in the Virgin Birth. When some of the ministers began to question the young man more severely, an older minister stood up and said he hoped they would not make a big point of this because he did not accept it, either.

"Why not?" someone asked.

"Because it is only found on two pages of the New Testament. Matthew and Luke are the only ones who ever mention it. In all of the writings of Paul, he never introduces the question of the Virgin Birth."

Dr. Rimmer rose to his feet and said, "Tell us then, what do you teach and preach?"

The older minister answered, "The Sermon on the Mount. That's enough for anyone."

Dr. Rimmer said it was not enough for him, because "he didn't believe in the Sermon on the Mount."

That hit like a bombshell in the midst of the Presbytery.

"Why ever not?" asked the old minister.

"Because it only occurs on two pages of the New Testament and Matthew and Luke are the only Gospels who mention it," retorted Dr. Rimmer.

The old minister was taken aback by that line of reasoning, the same he had been using, of course, to negate the idea of the Virgin Birth of Christ.

The "argument from silence" is next to no argument at all. It is the worst of all possible arguments because with it you can prove or disprove almost anything. For example, it's true that Mark never mentions the Virgin Birth of Christ. It is also true that Mark never mentions the birth of Christ at all. Ergo, Mark didn't believe that Jesus had ever been born. Isn't logic wonderful? The same strained logic of the "argument from silence" could say that because Paul did not mention any of the miracles or parables of Jesus, then obviously Paul never believed that Jesus worked miracles or told parables. The "argument from silence" has been long refuted by anyone who thinks clearly.

The third reason many reject the Virgin Birth is that stories of miraculous and virgin births are found in heathen legends. Therefore, they say, the biblical story of the Virgin Birth was taken from these earlier pagan mythologies and religions. Let's look at a few of the most prominent:

- Greek mythology teaches that Zeus, the Greek god, came into Alcmene and produced Hercules.

- Vish, in his eighth incarnation or avatar, came out as the virgin-born Krishna.

- Buddha is supposed to have been born of his mother, Maya, in a virgin birth.

- Augustus Caesar and Alexander the Great both claimed to have had virgin births.

Skeptics say that clearly the story of the Virgin Birth of Christ was stolen from these pagan religions and is to be dumped into the same dust heap of history with all of the rest of them.

Before we do that, let's take a closer look at the quality of these stories:

- In the case of Zeus and Hercules, we discover what we see among the Greek gods all the time. The Greek gods are simply men blown up large with all of their sins and foibles, cohabitating with human beings. Behind each such story is lust and lasciviousness of the "gods" in their desire for some fair mortal woman.

- In the case of Vishnu, he had first, supposedly, been incarnated as a fish, a turtle, a boar, a lion, and other bizarre things.

- As to Buddha, his mother says that a six-tusked white elephant with red veins came into her side and produced him.

- In the case of Augustus Caesar, he claims that his mother, Olympia, was impregnated by a serpent.

By the way, Alexander the Great made the same claim—that his father was a snake, something I wouldn't want to boast about.

Look at these stories. What a difference there is between the chaste and pure record of the Virgin Birth of Christ by the Holy Spirit and these depraved and bizarre stories of pagan religions.

Let's put an ax to the root of the tree of this argument. The thrust of the argument is that these stories antedate the story of the Virgin Birth of Christ found in Matthew and Luke, and that the two Gospel writers stole them from these earlier stories. But that is not the case. The fact of the matter is that the story of the Virgin Birth is found in Isaiah 7:14, where God says He will give them a sign: "Behold, a virgin shall conceive and bear a son, and shall call his name Immanuel," the fulfillment of which is described by Matthew. This was seven hundred years before Christ, which antedates all but a few of these pagan religion stories.

But let's go back farther to discover the Protoevangelium, *the first Gospel,* that wondrous promise given by God to our first parents in Eden—the only Utopia that man has ever known. Disaster fell. They sinned and disobeyed God. Sin had entered like venom into the veins of the human race and offered nothing but death by sin. In the midst of that stygian blackness there appeared a single star, a star of prophetic hope, *a star of promise,* the Protoevangelium. God said that the seed of the woman would destroy the head of the serpent, even though the serpent would wound the heel of the seed of the woman. In all of Scripture, there is no other person called the "seed of the woman," which points to a virgin birth. Everyone is begotten by man, as we can see in the chronologies of Christ found in Matthew.

It is even written large by God in the stars. All twelve signs of the Zodiac are taken from Genesis 3:15—the Protoevangelium. They are all pictures of the seed of the woman coming from Virgo, the virgin, who will destroy the head of the serpent, pictured in various ways, as a serpent, a scorpion, a dragon, and so on, all slain by the great heroes.

But then, in the time of the regnancy of Babylon, when polytheism spread throughout the pagan world, the hopeful story of the Protoevangelium was distorted into the various pagan gods of antiquity, and the true meaning was lost. God had written it large. The gospel, with its core truth of the Virgin Birth, was preached unto all the world under heaven, even in the stars. It passed, albeit in distorted ways, into virtually every mythology of the nations of the world. The pagan stories were simply perverted recollections of the great truth that God revealed from the beginning in the Protoevangelium. So, rather than the heathen legends being the source of the biblical concept of the Virgin Birth of Christ, it is the biblical concept of the Virgin Birth preannounced in the Protoevangelium in Genesis 3 that is the source of all the pagan mythological views. Instead of refuting the concept of the Virgin Birth, they establish it.

A young man, newly minted from seminary, was sent out to preach in a small country church. The Scandinavian folk who lived there came to hear him. There was an old farmer who was a skeptic and something of a curmudgeon who didn't come to church at all. The young man invited him, even offering to pick him up, so the farmer accepted. The young man preached that morning on the Virgin Birth. On the way home, he said to the old farmer, "Well, what did you think of the sermon?"

Mr. Worldly Wise of the Sod said, "Well, now, son, if some girl today got herself pregnant, had a baby, and then told you it was a virgin birth, would you believe it?"

The young man pondered for a moment, then said, "Well, yes, I would—if that baby grew up to live like Christ."

Science demands that every effect has a sufficient and adequate cause. In a world where everyone has sinned, where there are none righteous, where the heart is deceitful above all things, where the front pages of the newspapers all over the world, every day, morning and night, proclaim the sinfulness of man, they are only underscoring the truth of Genesis 3. Man fell!

Yet in the midst of that mud heap, there grew a single, solitary, pure Lily. How do we explain it? Every effect must have an adequate or sufficient cause. The only adequate cause is the fact of the Virgin Birth, that He didn't inherit the venom of sin that has poisoned the human race. The uniqueness of Christ demands a unique birth.

Beyond these scientific investigations, arguments, and debates by "pebble-droppers," I believe the Virgin Birth is true because Christ arose from the dead. That takes it out of the personal and private and puts it into the objective, the real, and the public. The resurrection of Christ is the most firmly attested fact of antiquity. Therefore, all the evidence to the resurrection of Christ is evidence for the Virgin Birth of Jesus. Why? Because the Scripture tells us that when God raised Him from the dead, He put His imprimatur upon the atonement of Jesus Christ and declared that the sacrifice had been accepted. The sacrifice would not have been accepted if Christ were not pure, and He would not have been pure if He were born a sinner like all of us.

The Virgin Birth is obviously something of a subjective nature—a very personal, private matter—known ultimately only by Mary. Still, we might add one more proof from Mary herself. Mary could have stopped the Crucifixion. Very simply, she could have stopped the torture and the agony of her son's death on the cross. How? He was crucified for one reason: He claimed that God was His Father.

If that were a lie, if Mary had been unchaste, she would have had to admit that she was immoral, but she could have stepped forward at any time and said, "Stop this horror! I'm ashamed! I confess! I will tell you who His real Father is!" She could have destroyed His whole pretensions and saved Him from the cross.

No mother, to save her own reputation, would allow her son to be horribly mutilated and killed. Mary could have and would have stopped her son's horrible death, as any mother would have, except that she knew who His Father was.

She knew Jesus' Father was God.

No, Jesus is the virgin-born, divine Son of God, the Redeemer of men. And what we need to ask ourselves today, is whether the virgin-born One has been born in us. It is still and eternally true that "though Christ a thousand times in Bethlehem be born, if He be not born in thee, thy soul is still forlorn."

CHAPTER TEN

WHY I BELIEVE IN THE RESURRECTION

To whom also he showed himself alive after his passion by many infallible proofs being seen of them forty days, and speaking of the things pertaining to the kingdom of God.

ACTS 1:3

Since the beginning of time, men and women have responded to the death of loved ones with a cry like that of Job: "If a man die, shall he live again?" (14:14). Human philosophy and pagan religions have been able to answer with no more than a question mark, a wish, or a vague hope.

The great genius of Greek philosophy, Plato, was asked: "Shall we live again?" His response: "I hope so, but no man may know." The tombs of Muhammad or Buddha or Confucius are occupied, but the tomb of Christ is empty to this day.

Why then do we believe in the resurrection of Christ,

129

this most important of all Christian doctrines, beside which all other doctrines are relatively insignificant? Even the cross of Christ without the Resurrection symbolizes simply that One who was rejected, that One who was hanged and accursed by God. But it is by the Resurrection that Christ is declared the Son of God with power, and it is by the Resurrection that His atoning sacrifice is declared to be accepted by God. This is the center of the Christian faith. With it everything stands or falls. Therefore all skeptics through nineteen centuries have aimed their largest guns at the resurrection of Jesus Christ.

The evidence for the resurrection of Jesus Christ has been examined more carefully than the evidence for any other fact of history! It has been weighed and considered by the greatest of scholars, among them Simon Greenleaf, the Royal professor of law at Harvard from 1833 to 1848 who helped bring Harvard Law School to preeminence and who has been called the greatest authority on legal evidences in the history of the world. When Greenleaf turned his mind upon the resurrection of Christ and focused upon it the light of all the laws of evidence, he concluded that the resurrection of Christ was a reality, that it was a historical event, and that anyone who examined the evidence for it honestly would be convinced this was the case.[1] So it was with Frank Morison, a British lawyer who set out to write a book repudiating the resurrection of Jesus Christ. He wrote his book, but it was not the book he set out to write. As he examined the evidence for the resurrection of Christ, this skeptical lawyer found it so overwhelming he was forced to accept it and become a believer. The book he did write, titled *Who Moved the Stone?*, sets forth the evidence for the resurrection of Christ, and its first chapter is called "The Book That Refused to Be Written." Lew Wallace also set out to write a book disproving the deity of Christ and His resurrection and ended up writing a famous book defending it. That book was titled *Ben Hur*.

The evidence for the resurrection of Christ, in the minds of those who have taken time to examine it, is very, very significant. I have met many people who do not believe in the resurrection of Christ, but I have never met one person who has read even a single book on the evidences for the Resurrection who did not believe it.

Let us consider what some of these evidences are. There is the fact of the Lord's Day. For thousands of years the Hebrew people had held their Sabbath doctrine. Then we find a group of early Christians who were Jews changing the day of worship from the seventh to the first day! What could account for their abandoning something to which they had held so tenaciously? Nothing other than such a monumental event as the resurrection of Christ from the dead, which took place on the first day of the week; His appearance to His disciples on the first day of the week; and the outpouring of His Spirit on the church at Pentecost on the first day of the week. So we read that it was on the first day of the week that the disciples of Jesus Christ met to worship Him.

Then there is the fact of Easter. This was a replacement of the Jewish festival of the Passover. Why did the Jews who held the Passover to be the most significant event in the history of their nation abandon it in favor of the celebration of

Easter, which was the festival of festivals among the Christians? The greeting was: "Christ is risen!" And the response: "Christ is risen indeed!" What other fact than that of the Resurrection can explain the existence of the festival of Easter, which traces itself all the way back to the time of the early church?

There is the fact of the Christian sacraments, which point not only to the death and suffering of Christ but also to His resurrection and power. These can be traced back in unbroken succession to the very time of the death of Jesus Christ.

There is the fact of Christian art. In the catacombs of Rome, from the time of the persecutions, we find carved into the walls representations of the resurrection of Christ as a part of the very earliest beliefs of the Christians.

There is also the fact of Christian hymnody. In the earliest days of the Christian church, hymns were sung to the resurrected Jesus Christ.

Then there is the undeniable fact of the Christian church. Many people do not make the connection between the church and the Resurrection, but all scholars have. The Christian church is the largest institution that exists or has ever existed in the history of the world. The Christian church is five times larger than the Roman Empire at its greatest extent. More than one billion three hundred million people this day profess to worship Jesus Christ as the living and risen Son of God. How did such an institution come into existence? As someone said: "The Grand Canyon was not formed by an Indian dragging a stick." Neither was an institution the size of the Christian church brought to pass by the daydreams of idle dreamers in days gone by. It is known by all historians that the Christian church can be traced back to the city of Jerusalem in A.D. 30, the time of the death and resurrection of Christ.

You can peruse H. G. Wells's *Outline of History* and other secular history books and find that generally they tell the story of the life and death of Jesus Christ. Then a new chapter begins telling of the rise of the Christian church and the disciples' preaching, and somehow there is a connection between those two chapters. It is an indisputable fact of history, not faith, that the largest institution in the history of the world began in A.D. 30 in Jerusalem when the apostles began to preach that Jesus Christ rose from the dead. The very heart and substance of the message of the early Christians was that Christ was risen from the dead. The first message delivered at Pentecost was entirely about the resurrection of Christ: about the prophecies that went before it in the Old Testament; about the fact that they had crucified the Lord of glory and God had raised Him from the dead; about the fact that they were the witnesses of these things; about the fact that the risen Christ had now poured out His spirit; and about the fact that because He was risen, He could grant the remission of sins to those who would believe in Him.

All the Scripture and the testimony of unbelievers and hostile enemies of Christianity as well declare that the church was spread everywhere because of this teaching that Christ had risen from the dead. It is a fact that the church of Jesus Christ came into being because the apostles declared that He rose from the dead.

Three alternatives are possible: (1) this was fraud, and the apostles lied; (2) they were deluded, deceived, and in error; (3) Christ did rise from the dead. Let us consider the efforts that have been made by skeptics to deny the fact of the Resurrection.

In more than twenty years of studying the resurrection, I have found that it is like an island guarded by all sorts of reefs positioned around it in concentric circles. Any ship that attempts to get through to destroy that island will be grounded on one or another of those reefs. Only a handful of theories have been propounded by skeptics, atheists, and unbelievers who have turned their greatest guns upon the Resurrection. All one has to do to be even more convinced about the resurrection of Christ is to examine these theories to see how vain they are. *The Cause and Cure of Infidelity* by Dr. David Nelson records that as a young man in college and graduate school he lost his faith but was still upset by an uneasy conscience. In order to bolster himself in his unbelief, he read the writings of all the greatest atheists. He had enough mental acumen to see that their arguments were so fatuous and empty that they would not hold water. This led to his conversion to Jesus Christ.

We are confronted with the fulfillment of the prophecies of the resurrection of Christ in the Old Testament; of the predictions of Christ Himself that He would be taken and scourged and would be crucified, and on the third day would rise again from the dead. If we suppose that He was involved in some conspiracy, we are confronted with the character of Jesus Christ Himself—this man whom the whole world joins together to declare to be the greatest, the most ethical, the most pure, the most honest man the world has ever known. We are confronted with the empty tomb—that rock upon which many a theory has gone aground. We are confronted with the graveclothes; with the testimony of the witnesses; with the twelve different occasions when Christ appeared to people, with more than five hundred people who saw Him risen; with the nature of these appearances in the morning and afternoon and evening, inside and outside, in which they handled and touched Him; with the tremendous transformation of the apostles from fearful, timid cowards to bold proclaimers of the gospel. The apostle Peter, who one day was afraid of a little maiden, was a few days later confronting the whole Sanhedrin, affirming to them that he could not but declare that which he had seen and heard. Then we have the faithfulness, the character, the suffering, and the death of these witnesses, most of whom sealed their testimony with their blood.

This is a vitally important fact. In the history of psychology it has never been known that a person was willing to give up life for what he or she knew to be a lie. I used to wonder why it was that God allowed the apostles and all the early Christians to go through such suffering, such tremendous unbelievable tortures. The foundations of Christianity are so established that they are absolutely unshakable today. Paul Little said, "Men will die for what they believe to be true, though it may actually be false. They do not, however, die for what they know is a lie."[2]

There are the fact and the testimony of Christ's ascension. There is the undeniable fact of the tremendous conversion and transformation of the apostle Paul—from Saul, the persecutor and murderer of Christians, to Paul, the greatest apostle in the history of Christianity.

Let us consider some of the various theories that try to explain away the Resurrection. In the area of fraud, there is the idea that either the disciples themselves, or the disciples in conjunction with Jesus Christ, conspired to deceive the world into believing that He had risen from the dead. This was the earliest theory to be set forth. It is found even in the Bible when the guards came into Jerusalem and reported to the Sanhedrin (the ruling body of the Jews) that the tomb was empty and all the things that had transpired. The Sanhedrin gave the guards large sums of money and said: "Say ye, His disciples came by night, and stole him away while we slept. And if this come to the governor's ears, we will persuade him, and secure you" (Matthew 28:13–14). In the entire history of jurisprudence there has never under any circumstances been a witness who has been allowed to testify to what transpired while he was asleep. "While we were asleep, the apostles came." For a Roman soldier to fall asleep on guard duty meant inevitably the death penalty. And this was rigorously applied.

The Scottish theologian Dr. Principal Hill commented on this idea of falsehood in what I think is a classic quote. He said, after examining all the evidence, "But if not withstanding every appearance of truth, you suppose their testimony to be false, then inexplicable circumstances of glaring absurdity crowd upon you. You must suppose that twelve men of mean birth, of no education, living in that humble station which placed ambitious views out of their reach and far from their thoughts, without any aid from the state, formed the noblest scheme which ever entered into the mind of man, adopted the most daring means of executing that scheme, and conducted it with such address as to conceal the imposture under the semblance of simplicity and virtue. You must suppose that men guilty of blasphemy and falsehood, united in an attempt the best contrived, and which has in fact proved the most successful, for making the world virtuous; that they formed this singular enterprise without seeking any advantage to themselves, with an avowed contempt of loss and profit, and with the certain expectation of scorn and persecution; that although conscious of one another's villainy, none of them ever thought of providing for his own security by disclosing the fraud, but that amidst sufferings the most grievous to flesh and blood they persevered in their conspiracy to cheat the world into piety, honesty and benevolence. Truly, they who can swallow such suppositions have no title to object to miracles."[3]

Lawyer Frank Morison says: "We have to account not merely for the enthusiasm of its friends [of the church], but for the paralysis of its enemies and for the ever-growing stream of new converts which came over to it. When we remember what certain highly placed personages in Jerusalem would almost certainly have given to have strangled this movement at its birth but could not—how one desperate expedient after another was adopted to silence the apostles, until that veritable bow of Ulysses, the Great Persecution, was tried and broke in pieces in their hands—we begin to realize that behind all these subterfuges and makeshifts there must have stood a silent, unanswerable fact, a fact which geography and the very fates themselves had made immovable. We realize also why it was that throughout the four years when Christianity was growing to really formidable dimensions in Jerusalem, neither Caiaphas nor Annas, nor any recognized member of the Sadducean camarilla, whose prestige and personal repute was so deeply affronted and outraged by the new doctrine, ever took the obvious shortcut out of their difficulties."[4] If the body of Jesus still lay in the tomb in which Joseph had deposited it, or if they themselves had taken it and placed it somewhere else, why did they not say so? No, they were paralyzed and totally incapable of doing anything about it. Their only expedient was the Great Persecution.

Some have said that the Resurrection was a legend that just gradually grew up. This was a popular theory in the last century when the higher critics said that the Gospels were written a hundred or two hundred years after the events, but the advance of archaeology has silenced this criticism. Now we know that the Gospels go right back to the authors whose names they bear, and that the testimony of the Resurrection goes back to the very decade in which it took place. Therefore, there was no possible time for legend to develop. Furthermore, the legend had already developed at least sixteen years before Paul could say that there were five hundred people, most of whom were alive at that time, who had seen the resurrected Christ.

Still less tenable, perhaps, is the vision theory. This speculates that the appearances of the resurrected Christ were simply visions or hallucinations brought about by the great expectations these people had that Jesus would rise from the dead. If that were the case, how do we account for the fact that the women came to the tomb bearing spices? Were they to anoint a risen Christ or a dead body? How do we account for the fact that Mary sat outside the tomb weeping because her Lord was dead and the corpse had been stolen? How do we account for the fact that the two on the road to Emmaus were totally disconsolate and dejected because they had thought the crucified Christ was the Messiah who should have delivered Israel, but now were convinced everything was lost? How do we account for the unbelief of the disciples in the Upper Room where Jesus rebuked them for their disbelief? No, they were not expecting a resurrected Christ!

In the history of hallucinations there is no incident in which five hundred people from different backgrounds, of different temperaments, ever saw the same vision at the same time! Furthermore, there are innumerable other reefs upon which that ship will go aground. If these were simply hallucinations that they were seeing, did none of the disciples think about going to the tomb to see if the body was still there? When they proclaimed their "hallucinations," did none of their enemies ever consider taking a few steps over to examine the tomb? When Peter preached at Pentecost about his "great hallucination," he was only ten minutes away from the tomb. Thousands of people believed; other thousands heard and did not believe. Did no one think of walking down the street to check it out? Hardly! Certainly those sophisticated, conspiring Sadducees would have taken every opportunity to show that this was simply a hallucination.

Last, there is the "swoon" theory. This has been set forth by Venturini; it is found in the writings of Mary Baker Eddy; it is found in the writings of Hugh Schonfield in *The Passover Plot*. It is interesting, however, that for more than eighteen hundred years there was never a whisper from the friends or the most implacable enemies of Christianity that Jesus Christ had not died. Some of these recent writers have now conceived the idea that Jesus had simply swooned, was taken down from the cross and thought to be dead; then, in the coolness of the tomb, He revived and came out and convinced His disciples that He had risen from the dead. That ship would never have gotten within a hundred miles of our resurrection island.

Consider these facts: Ignored is the wound from the centurion—delivered into the side with a Roman spear, producing both blood and water—empirical evidence that life had ceased, because the blood had separated into its constituent elements. There is the testimony of the centurion who was sent by Pilate, a man who dealt and trafficked in death, whose business it was as an executioner to know that Jesus was dead. Then there was the fact of the graveclothes. The Jews wrapped bodies in these graveclothes and used a hundred pounds of spices between the folds, sealing those clothes around the corpse, mummylike. The head was also wrapped. Medical authorities state that if Jesus had swooned, open air was needed, not a closed tomb. Certainly what was not needed were graveclothes wrapped around His head and spices covering His nose and mouth. Furthermore, to place a person in such a swoon in a cold grave would bring about a syncope or cessation of his heartbeat, if he had been alive.

Suppose He did extricate Himself from these graveclothes, without in any way disturbing them, and then go to the huge stone that sealed the tomb. He would have had to move it with hands that had been pierced with the large Roman spikes used for crucifixions. He would have had to place them on the flat inside of this enormous stone and simply roll it away. Greek terms in the Gospels indicate that it was rolled uphill. Indeed, that is a miraculous feat in itself! He then would have had to overcome a Roman armed guard and walk fourteen miles that afternoon to Emmaus and back. That was to loosen up His feet after the spikes had pierced them, to get in shape for His walk all the way to the north of Palestine to Galilee where He climbed a mountain!

The famous critic David Strauss, who did not believe in the Resurrection but also did not believe in such nonsense as the "swoon" theory, said: "It is impossible that one who had just come forth from the grave, half dead who crept about weak and ill, who stood in need of medical treatment, of bandaging, strengthening and tender care, and who at last succumbed to suffering, could ever have given to the disciples the impression that He was a conqueror over death and the grave—that He was the Prince of Life—[an impression] which lay at the bottom of their future ministry. Such a resuscitation could only have weakened the impression which He had made upon them in life and in death."[5]

Consider the ascension of Jesus Christ. Did this One who had managed to resuscitate Himself and get out of the tomb also fly up into the sky? This is what the disciples affirmed. Or are we to involve the disciples in this fraud? Remember they subsequently gave their lives in horrible deaths. No. All the theories that have been propounded fall into the dust as we examine facts so evident that no one has ever been able to refute them.

The empty tomb is admitted not only by the friends but also by the foes of Christianity. The Roman guard admitted it; the Sanhedrin tacitly admitted it by telling the soldiers to say that His disciples had stolen Him.

Trypho, one of the earliest and greatest Jewish apologists, in a dialogue with Justin Martyr speaks of "one Jesus, a Galilean deceiver, whom we crucified; but his disciples stole him by night from the tomb, where he was laid when unfastened from the cross, and now deceive men by asserting that he has arisen from the dead and ascended into heaven."[6] So even Trypho admits the tomb was empty, setting forth the theory that the disciples stole the body, a theory nobody believes today.

There is the final fact of Christian experience: that this risen Jesus Christ has gone throughout all the world and that He has reached down and transformed human beings in every nation, tongue, and tribe of this earth; that countless millions of people have come to know that He is alive from the dead and has come to enter their lives and transform them. He is the One who says: "I am he that liveth and who was dead; and behold, I am alive for evermore. . . . Whosoever liveth and believeth in me shall never die" (Revelation 1:18; John 11:26).

Even now Christ stands knocking at the door of our hearts and He says, "If any man hear my voice and open the door I will come in to him and will sup with him, and he with me" (Revelation 3:20). Unless we have come to know Him experientially in the laboratory of our own souls, we are without hope in this world and the world to come. For Jesus and His resurrection are the only hope of mankind. Without that, we have nothing to look forward to but a black hole in the ground.

Christ is risen, indeed! He is alive, as He said, and He is willing to come and live in our hearts if we are willing to repent of our sins and place our trust in Him who died for us and rose again.

CHAPTER ELEVEN

WHY I BELIEVE IN CHRISTIANITY

Therefore if any man be in Christ, he is a new creature: old things are passed away; behold, all things are become new.

2 CORINTHIANS 5:17

I do not believe that it is enough merely to believe in Christ and the Bible. It is also necessary that we believe that Christianity has been a boon to mankind, that it has had a beneficent effect upon the human race. That opinion is not held by everyone. The redoubtable Madalyn Murray O'Hair, for example, has said that nothing good has ever come from Christianity. If Christianity has not done good and produced good, then we must reject it regardless of anything else. Even Christ taught: "Ye shall know them by their fruits" (Matthew 7:16).

What are the facts and the fruits of the Christian faith? Christianity teaches that the human race is depraved, fallen, and sinful, and that even the greatest of saints is still impure and sinful. First of all, then, we should keep in mind that we have this treasure in earthen vessels, and there has never been a perfect reflection of Jesus Christ in the life of any of His followers.

Second, we must remember that Christianity has often been blamed for things that true Christians did not do, and that those who profess do not necessarily possess what they profess. For example, perhaps the darkest blotch and accusation that could be brought against Christianity would be the Spanish Inquisition. I would not endeavor to defend it. It was deplorable in the highest degree, a monstrous epic of brutality and barbarity. It was diabolical in its nature.

Was this Christians persecuting non-Christians? It was the very opposite. I am quite convinced that the members of the Inquisitorial Party were not Christians. They lived in the Dark Ages when the gospel of Jesus Christ had been all but totally forgotten, and the faith so perverted that it bore little resemblance to that which had been given by Christ. In many cases the victims of the Inquisition were evangelical Protestant Christians who had come to realize what the historic gospel of Christ was and who had rejected the papal superstitions of that time. These were the people who were exposed to these tremendous tortures.

The Pit and the Pendulum, a magnificent book by Edgar Allan Poe, is a picture of the Spanish inquisitors of the Roman church pouring out all of their exquisite tortures on an English Protestant. The truth about the Inquisition is that these were spurious Christians, men who were Christian in name only, persecuting those who were real. When understood, to denounce the Inquisition is not a real attack on

Christianity. I am quite certain that no Christian would ever torture anyone.

What has Christianity accomplished? First, we should notice that since Christianity came into the world, it has become a world force. In 1980 it numbered almost three times the size of its nearest rival. This came about against the most staggering odds when one considers that Christianity is the proclamation of the death of a carpenter of Nazareth, who is claimed to be the Divine Creator of the world. Suppose that today in the cities of Europe or America missionaries were to appear telling us that just recently some obscure peasant had been put to death in Persia and was reputed to have risen from the dead and declared to be the eternal Creator of the cosmos. What chance to you think such missionaries would have in propagating such a religion? Can you not see that the probabilities against such a faith ever taking hold would be staggering? But this is precisely what the apostles did in the Roman Empire, and amazing as it is, they succeeded in overthrowing that pagan empire. This feat simply demonstrates that in this absurd and incredible declaration there must have been inherent some supernatural power. It was indeed the very power of the Spirit of God, who reached down and drew unto Himself those whom He would by irresistible power.

Against all the opposition and persecution that could be mustered, Christianity continued to grow and flourish. Even the attempts of Julian the Apostate to overthrow Christianity and reestablish the pagan Roman religions met with no success. One of the emperor's followers said to a Christian when Julian's onslaught against Christianity was at its highest,

"What is your carpenter's son doing now?" To which the Christian replied, "He is making a coffin for your emperor." It was not long after this that Julian, mortally wounded in battle and falling on the ground, picked up the sand mingled with his blood, threw it into the air, and cried, "Thou hast conquered, O Galilean." And the march of Christianity surged on.

Waves of diabolical torture swept the Roman Empire in a Satan-inspired effort to purge the world of the newborn Christian faith. Yet, the blood of the martyrs became the seed of the church, and Christ continued on His way, conquering and to conquer. Soon a Christian was placed on the throne of Rome, and the mightiest empire the world had ever seen collapsed before the gospel of the Galilean carpenter. Its ameliorating work began upon the pagan world.

Many people today who live in an ostensibly Christian environment with Christian ethics do not realize how much we owe Jesus of Nazareth. The world into which He was born was an altogether different world from ours, and, without His coming, the world would be an altogether different place from the one we know today. What goodness and mercy there is in this world have come in large measure from Him.

Consider the gladiatorial fights. Hundreds of thousands of slaves shed their blood in the arena in Rome year after year to satisfy the perverted lusts of the Roman mob. One day a Christian by the name of Telemachus leaped into the arena between two armed gladiators and held them apart. At a sign from the emperor, he was pierced with their swords and fell to the ground. But by sacrificing his life he spared the lives of hundreds of thousands of others. There was no cry of glee from the crowd. They looked at this saintly man lying dead in his blood, and a silence came over that vast arena. They went out shamefacedly, and that was the end of the gladiatorial shows in Rome. Jesus Christ had given a worth and significance to every life: "Are ye not worth much more than these?"

The child of today is loved and adored. But it was not so in pre-Christian times. The Roman father's power over his child was absolute. He could expose it to death; he could scourge it, mutilate it, marry it, divorce it, sell it as a slave, or kill it to satisfy his own blood lust. Quintilian, a Roman writer, said that to kill a man was often held to be a crime, but to kill one's own children was sometimes considered a beautiful action among the Romans. Tacitus, the great Roman writer, tells us of the pathetic pictures of newborn children who were taken on the first day of their lives and left on the mountainside, exposed to wild beasts, or to those strange people who flitted around in the dark to seize these children for even more perverse and horrible destinies and dents. Jesus Christ took a little child in His arms and blessed it, and infanticide began to melt away from the world.

What about the state of women in that day? In the heathen world the condition of women was no less dismal than that of children. Women were of very little esteem until Jesus came. The writings of the Hindus, the Brahminical writings, state that a woman is never fit for independence; women have no business with the scriptures of the Hindus; and sinful women must be as foul as falsehood itself.

Robert Ingersoll, a great skeptic who lectured against the

Bible, had the temerity at one time to make a statement that women were better off in heathen lands than they were in Christian lands. Consider the state of women in heathen lands. The traveler Commander Cameron witnessed in the center of Africa the death of a chieftain and the usual practice that ensued. First the tribal members diverted the course of a river and in its bed dug an enormous pit, the bottom of which was then covered with living women. At one end a woman was placed on her hands and knees and upon her back was seated the dead chief, covered with beads and other treasures, being supported by one of his wives, while the second wife sat at his feet. The earth was then shoveled in upon them and all the women were buried alive with the exception of the second wife. For her, the custom was merciful for she had the privilege of being killed before being buried. Or consider the grotesque Indian custom of Suttee: Whenever a husband died the woman was burned alive with the body of her husband.

The condition of the slave in the ancient world was even worse. Half of the entire Roman Empire consisted of slaves. The city of Athens had four hundred thousand inhabitants; one hundred thousand of those were free and three hundred thousand were slaves. Slavery in the ancient world was far more brutal than anything modern slavery has demonstrated. One Roman had six hundred slaves put to death for the killing of a man. Another Roman master put a slave to death simply for the pleasure of a guest who had never seen anyone die.

What brought an end to ancient slavery? It was the gospel of Jesus Christ! It was that small letter the apostle Paul wrote to Philemon. A runaway slave had been thrown into a Roman prison with the apostle Paul, and Paul had converted him to Christ. When released, Paul sent him back to Philemon. The custom at that time was to kill an escaped slave after he had been recaptured. Philemon had also become a Christian— another convert of the apostle Paul. Paul said to Philemon: "Receive him . . . not now as a servant, but above a servant, a brother" (Philemon 15–16). In that new brotherhood in Jesus Christ that was being produced throughout the Roman world slavery found its death knell.

One year before the Protestant Reformation of 1517, slavery was revived again by Spain and Portugal. It was the slavery of the newly discovered blacks. What happened to it? We know that slavery was first abolished in England through William Wilberforce, who had been converted by the preaching of Wesley. Wilberforce, a small hunchbacked man, became one of the most powerful of all of England's prime ministers. Consumed with the gospel of Christ and with the freedom that Jesus brought, this man devoted all his energy and eloquence to the overthrow of the obnoxious African slave trade. His success in abolishing slavery throughout the British Empire led to agitation for such action in this country. Through the proclamations that thundered from the pulpits of the North, the abolitionist parties came into being and succeeded finally in destroying slavery in America.

Probably nothing in the annals of human history compares to what has been accomplished by Christian missions. A writer who returned one hundred and thirty or so years ago to England from a trip around the world found that missions and missionaries were being bombarded with criticism in the

London papers. So he wrote a letter to the paper defending missions; he said the transformation of wild savages in the isles of the South Seas was something to behold, and to make light of this was a heinous crime: "In a voyager to forget these things is base ineptitude; for should he chance to be at the point of shipwreck on some unknown coast, he will most devoutly pray that the lesson of the missionary may have preceded him."[1] The author of that letter to the newspaper was Charles Darwin. After his return from his around-the-world trip he was transformed. Whether the missionaries had been there or not would probably make the difference between being invited to dinner or being the dinner.

The Papuans, one of the aboriginal tribes of Australia, were considered by some evolutionists to be so primitive that they had less mind than a crow. Yet missionaries from Holland began to work with them. For many years they met defeat and discouragement, as not one single Papuan accepted Christ. Finally in 1860 the firstfruits of the New Holland Mission were seen when a man named Nathaniel Pepper, one of the Papuan aborigines, accepted Jesus Christ. Some years later, when thousands had been converted, the Papuan school won first prize in academic competitions among the twelve hundred colonial schools in New Holland. Quite a feat for those with the brains of a crow!

Skeptics have done little for the savage. They have built few leprosariums, few hospitals, few orphanages. It has remained for the followers of Jesus Christ to care for the offscouring of mankind.

Christianity has brought to the world liberty and freedom. In every ancient state, the state was supreme and the individual was nothing; the individual's only significance was to serve the state. In modern times where the gospel of Christ has been banished and atheism is again regnant (as in communist lands), the same ancient pagan doctrine is back in force. But where the Spirit of Christ is, there is liberty, and Jesus is the One who gave individuals their worth.

The Son of God came from heaven and gave His life for me and for you and for all others. And men and women felt their worth and their need for freedom. Wherever the gospel has gone, it has been a leavening force to end dictatorships and to bring about freedom. Particularly notable in overthrowing tyranny and establishing freedom of worship is that form of Christianity known as the Reformed Faith, or Calvinism. A great source of power toward freedom and liberty, it has brought about many of the republics, limited monarchies, and democracies of this world—in Switzerland, in England, in Scotland, in America, and in many other nations.

The Mayflower Compact, that first document of the New World, begins in this way: "Having undertaken for the glory of God and the advancement of the Christian faith . . ." I am afraid that we have departed far from that original intention. Consider the various documents that were framed for the founding of the different colonies. Rhode Island, 1638: "We, whose names are underwritten do here solemnly in the presence of Jehovah, incorporate ourselves into a body politic and as He shall help, will submit our persons, our lives, and estates unto our Lord Jesus Christ, the King of kings and Lord of Lords. And to all those perfect and most absolute laws of His given us in His holy word of truth to be guided and judged thereby." Those who wish to separate the Bible from the state will have to take it out of the charter of many of our early states. Freedom is one of the gifts of Christianity.

I believe the Christian faith is the only force impeding and preventing the total disappearance of freedom in the world today. Communism recognized that the church of Christ was its most implacable foe. That is why the first of the ten commandments of the Comsomol (the world youth communist movement) stated that the number one enemy of communism was the Christian clergyman.

The head of the armed forces of South Korea realized that the North Koreans showed an incredible fear of a little black book called the New Testament. Therefore, he himself, though a Buddhist, ordered that every man in the armed forces of South Korea should be given a New Testament. The result was an enormous awakening in which several hundreds of thousands of soldiers were converted to Jesus Christ. The gospel of Christ is the salt of the earth that prevents utter corruption. That gospel is enshrined in the hearts of those who are believers.

What would it mean if every person in the United States were converted to Jesus Christ in reality? I do not mean the church member; I mean a twice-born child of God. "If any man is in Christ, he is a new creature: the old things are passed away; behold, new things have come" (2 Corinthians 5:17 NASB). It should mean that the jails would become empty; the courts would shut down; the bars would close; the pornographic stores and theaters would be without business. There would be no need for alarm devices in homes, or even locks on doors, because genuine Christians, born-again men and women, do not steal, kill, rape, or do any of the thousands of other things that make life so unpleasant in America today.

A hundred years or so ago, in the Far West, two atheists were traveling through a storm as night was falling. Desperate for shelter, they were fortunate to find a cabin in the wilderness. Its occupant, a grizzled, weather-beaten old mountain man, graciously allowed them to sleep in one of his two rooms. As they retired, they said to each other, "Surely this man will fall upon us when we are asleep and kill us and take whatever we have of value. Therefore one of us will keep watch through the night." So the first man began his watch as the other lay down to sleep. Peeking through the crack of the door, he saw the old man take down a worn Bible from the shelf and open it, put on his glasses, and begin to read. The atheist lay down next to his friend, who said, "I thought somebody had to watch the old man." The first man answered, "From anyone who reads the Bible we have nothing to fear." How true that is!

Progress has been the result of Christianity. Science, as one scientist said, could never have originated in any other culture. It could not possibly have originated in the Muslim culture because of its belief in fatalism, which absolutely prevents any concept of scientific progress. It could not have originated among the Buddhists or the Hindus of Asia because of their belief that the physical world is not real, that nothing exists but God, and that all this is merely imagination. Only in Christianity could science have come to be!

Only through Christianity did education come to the world. I recall reading a list of the literacy rates of the nations around 1900. At that time the Western civilization of America and Europe had not been smeared all over the world as it is today, so that Tokyo looks little different from New York. Rather, each civilization reflected its own indigenous culture. What are the results? All of the nations that would be called "pagan" had literacy rates from 0 to 20 percent. Those nations that could be classified as Roman Catholic—such as Spain, Italy, Mexico, and so on—had literacy rates between 40 and 60 percent. All of the nations that could be categorized as Protestant had literacy rates of between 96 and almost 100 percent. Why? Because of their belief in the Word of God and the necessity for children to learn to read so they could read the Word of God.

Who has gone down into the slums to rescue the derelict? It is the city mission, the YMCA, the settlement mission. Only Christians have given themselves for such people as these. Today with the advancing of the barbarians again and the removal of the Scriptures from much of this land and much of the world, we again see decay and corruption setting in.

You and I are the salt of the earth. We need to get the salt out of the shaker and be that which preserves the life and health and morality of society. In these critical days, I am very glad to be a part of the church of Jesus Christ and of that kingdom that shall never end. He came and He died and promised that those who would trust in Him, who would simply trust in His death for their salvation, will themselves be transformed and renewed and made into the preservative of society and the only hope of the future of mankind.

CHAPTER TWELVE

WHY I BELIEVE IN THE SECOND BIRTH

I tell you the truth, no one can see the kingdom of God unless he is born again.

JOHN 3:3 NIV

Along with John and Charles Wesley, the famous Anglican clergyman George Whitefield was much responsible for the transformation of England and the Great Awakening in America. In a letter to Benjamin Franklin, who used to delight to come and hear Whitefield speak, he said: "As I find you growing more and more famous in the learned world, I would recommend to your diligent and unprejudiced study the mystery of the new birth. It is a most important study, and, when mastered, will richly answer all your pains. I bid you, my friend, remember that One at whose bar we shall both presently appear hath solemnly declared that without it we shall in no wise see His kingdom."[1] A very wise recommendation to a man who is noted in the history of the world as being a wise man.

History, however, affords us no evidence that Franklin heeded those words.

Jesus Christ said, "Ye must be born again" (John 3:7). That, primarily, is why I believe in the second birth: because Christ stated it. He declared it boldly, imperiously—He asseverated it. "Except a man be born again, he cannot see the kingdom of God" (John 3:3). Therefore I would, as solemnly and as earnestly as Whitefield did, urge upon your hearts, minds, and consciences this day the question: Have you been born again?

Jesus Christ tells us that, unless we have been, we shall not only not enter but we will also never even see the kingdom of heaven. *Must,* it is said, is the word of a king; and Christ is the King of kings and the kingdom of God. And Christ says, "Ye must be born again." The theological doctrine is called *regeneration.* The message of the entire Bible could be summed up in three words: *creation* (or generation), *degeneration,* and *regeneration.* This is the message of the Bible from one end to the other. God made man perfect. Man fell into sin and must be re-created into the image of God by the power of God's Spirit working through the gospel of Jesus Christ.

Second, I believe in the new birth because not only did Christ teach it, but also everywhere throughout the Scripture, in the Old and New Testaments, it is consistently taught as a fact and a necessity. We are told that we are to be born of water and of the Spirit. It is described as a making alive. "You hath he quickened [made alive], who were dead in trespasses and sins" (Ephesians 2:1). It is a passing from death unto life. It is a resurrection from the dead. It is a beginning again. It is a bringing forth. It is being born of God. It is being begotten again—not of corruptible but of the incorruptible seed of the Word of God. It is being begotten again unto a living hope. It is the washing of regeneration and the renewing of the Holy Spirit.

In the Old Testament it is called the circumcision of the heart. "The LORD thy God will circumcise thine heart, and the heart of thy seed, to love the LORD thy God with all thine heart, and with all thy soul, that thou mayest live" (Deuteronomy 30:6). The Scripture says in the New Testament (1 Corinthians 16:22), "If any man love not the Lord Jesus Christ, let him be *Anathema Maranatha*"—two Aramaic words that mean: "let him be accursed until the Lord comes"; that is, if he did not in sincerity love the Lord Jesus Christ. Religiosity, piety, morality will not suffice. Unless we have hearts that have been transformed to love God in truth with all our hearts and souls, we shall not see God and we shall not live.

The Old Testament further describes regeneration in Ezekiel 36:26 as a giving of a new heart. "A new heart also will I give you, and a new spirit will I put within you: and I will take away the stony heart out of your flesh, and I will give you an heart of flesh"—a heart designed to love our God. The subjects of regeneration are said to be alive from the dead—to be new creatures—God's workmanship. "If any man be in Christ, he is a new creature: old things are passed away; behold, all things are become new" (2 Corinthians 5:17). Even as the serpent sloughs off its old skin and becomes completely new, so also the whole man, born spiritually dead, casts off his old life and becomes a new creature.

This doctrine has puzzled the hearts of billions of men.

They have pondered it in the night seasons in their own closets. Upon their beds they have wondered, *Is it true—is it possible that I can become a new person?* The Scripture clearly affirms that not only is it possible, but it is also absolutely essential. Christ taught it, the Scripture declares it, and all the creeds of the historic church of Christ affirm it. It is taught everywhere. The Westminster Confession of Faith, containing the doctrinal statements of the whole Presbyterian world, declares the belief that this true faith being wrought in man by the hearing of the Word of God and the operation of the Holy Spirit does regenerate and make him a new man, causing him to live a new life and freeing him from the bondage of sin. But it does not matter whether they are Presbyterian, Reformed, Anglican, Lutheran, Baptist, or Congregational— all of the symbols, creeds, and formalities of the church have expressly declared the necessity that man must be born again.

We also hear this declaration in our hymns at Christmastime. Particularly the thought is emphasized in "O Little Town of Bethlehem." We are familiar with the words from that hymn, "Be born in us today," or those in Charles Wesley's "Hark! the Herald Angels Sing" that tell us Christ came "to give [us] second birth." But untold millions of people have sung those words without the faintest knowledge of what they were singing.

Charles Spurgeon, the great English preacher of a century ago, said that natural man—the unregenerate—can no more understand what the new birth is, or what spiritual things are than a horse can understand astronomy. Imagine trying to teach astronomy to a horse! We might just as well try to teach the meaning of spiritual things to someone who has not been born of God's Spirit. For the Scripture declares: "The natural man receiveth not the things of the Spirit of God: for they are foolishness unto him: neither can he know them, because they are spiritually discerned" (2 Corinthians 2:14).

This is also taught in nature, in the snake's shedding of its skin or more dramatically in the caterpillar's metamorphosis. Crawling along the ground and the leaves, it eventually wraps itself in its dark cocoon, finally bursting forth from the chrysalis to become a beautiful butterfly floating in the breezes and lighting on the flowers. That caterpillar could no more understand the laws, the principles, and the life it one day will enter into than the unregenerate heart—the natural man—can understand what it is to be a spiritual person. So, I would ask again: Have you been born anew?

The second birth is also taught in all of the theologies, dictionaries, and compendiums of historical theological works. Thousands of theologians down through the centuries have taught that it is absolutely essential that man experience the fact of regeneration. Not only is it clearly taught on all sides, but the evidence is also plain to see, unless a person is willfully blinding her- or himself to it. All around us, down through twenty centuries, innumerable millions of people from every station in life have experienced this transforming power of the rebirth. They have become new creatures in their hearts and have been transformed from the very depths of their beings. All types of people—the great and the mighty; the base and the low; the noble and the ignoble; the savage and the sophisticate—have experienced the regenerating power of God and have thenceforth enjoyed the same new life in Christ.

Cyprian, a wealthy noble who lived in the third century, enjoyed galloping about Carthage in his gold and bejeweled chariot, wearing fancy clothes studded with diamonds and precious stones, living a debauched life. In a letter to one of the Christian theologians of the time, he said that he could not possibly conceive how he could change his life—the life he had lived for so long. The inveterate habits, tastes, and desires that he had developed, the sins that he clutched to his bosom, how could he ever possibly give these things up? How could he ever be like the Christians he saw? He said it seemed to him to be an utterly impossible thing; yet, in the mysterious providence of God, that which had seemed utterly impossible came to pass and Cyprian was transformed. God reached down from heaven and took out of Cyprian's breast that stony heart and placed within him a heart of flesh—a heart tuned to love his God and sing His praises. Cyprian, who became one of the great Christian leaders of the early church, said that the thing that before had seemed so utterly impossible and mysterious and difficult to understand had all become plain. All of his problems had disappeared.[2]

What would it be like to discuss with a caterpillar the problems of flight? It would seem so impossible—to flutter in the breeze, to light upon the flowers, to float into the sky. Why, that poor caterpillar could hardly jump a millimeter off the ground, and yet in the mysterious working of God all things become new—old things pass away, and a new creation is formed. In the same way, God makes a new heart in man.

The testimonies that this is so exist in hundreds and hundreds of famous people such as William Gladstone, one of England's greatest prime ministers whose life was transformed by God. Abraham Lincoln tells us in his letters that at Gettysburg, the day he delivered his famous address, he, too, was born again of God's Spirit. Luther had been exceedingly religious, even as Nicodemus was, and yet had known nothing of the new birth, but finally was transformed in his soul. Writers like Fyodor Dostoevski and Leo Tolstoi of Russia, for example, have described the work of God's Spirit in utterly transforming their lives. Men like Chuck Colson, author of the bestseller *Born Again*, and Harold E. Hughes, former senator from Iowa and author of *The Man from Ida Grove*, have told of being transformed by the Spirit of God. Indeed, the caterpillar has begun to fly because of the work of God's Spirit.

Most of all I believe in the new birth because I have experienced it. To this day I have friends from twenty-four years ago who do not know what happened to me. One moment there was a young man managing an Arthur Murray Dance Studio, his heart and affections fastened entirely upon the things of this world. Then suddenly, overnight, something happened: A new person was born and an old person died. Those things that once seemed so desirable, so compelling, now seemed as filthy rags, dead men's bones, things of no interest to me at all. Other things, the things of the kingdom of God, those things that are invisible, those eternal things that never occupied my thoughts at all and upon which my heart never dallied, have become exceedingly precious to me. Upon those things my affections have been fastened. You see, my friends, there is no other solution than that twenty-four years ago I was born all over again, as Jesus said. Have you been born again? You must, you know.

I remember the preacher who came to a church and on his first Sunday preached on this text, "Ye must be born again," and the people listened. Some squirmed. The following Sunday the preacher preached on the same text again, and the people were puzzled. The following week, he preached on the same text again. Finally some of the deacons said to him, "Pastor, why is it that every Sunday you preach on the same text, 'Ye must be born again'?" He replied, "Because you must."

My friends, this is the only thing that you must do during your stay on this planet—the only thing you must do. You don't have to even grow up. You don't have to succeed. You don't have to get married. You don't have to have children. You don't have to have a home, a car, and all of the things that people think they must have. The only thing that you must have is a rebirth because your entire future forever depends upon it. You must be born again. It is a divine imperative. It is a universal imperative. I think it is worthy of note that these words were uttered to Nicodemus—not to a Samaritan woman, not to a prostitute, not to a gambler, not to a profane man—but to a man who was a Pharisee and a ruler of the Jews. A Pharisee in that day, a member of the Sanhedrin, was a sort of combination of a minister and a senator all rolled up together, the elite of Israel. As an extraordinarily religious man, in the eyes of the people he would have been absolutely faultless, doing none of the things the sinners did. Yet Jesus said to Nicodemus, "Ye must be born again."

Christ is saying to us—Presbyterians, Methodists, Anglicans, Congregationalists, Roman Catholics, whatever we are—that except a man be born again, he shall in no wise enter into the kingdom of heaven. Now, we may ignore those words; millions have and millions will. But I assure you that one day the word of Jesus Christ will come to pass in that great Final Assize, when man shall stand before the judgment bar of God. It is very simple: Those who have received a new nature from God are those who will be admitted into heaven, and those who have not will not. That which is flesh is flesh. It is filled with the agents of its own destruction. Just so soon as death comes, so soon that horde of invaders is unleashed and within a few hours the corruption sets in. We must have a new and incorruptible birth.

The reason for the necessity of the new birth lies in the fact of the old death. For the Scripture plainly teaches that you and I and every person on this planet were born dead; we were stillborn, spiritually. We have been quickened, which were dead in trespasses and sin. Intellectually, emotionally, aesthetically, rationally, physically, yes, we were alive; but spiritually, we were born dead, and within us there exists a spirit that is dead and corrupt and stinks. God says we are a stench in His nostrils, and that He must come and with His life-giving fingers touch our souls and make us new again. There is an old spiritual axiom that many of the great theologians of the past repeated to impress upon people the necessity: The Bible not only teaches that there is a second birth, but it also teaches that there is a second death in addition to the physical death that we shall all endure. Those whose names are not found written in the Lamb's Book of Life will be cast into the lake of fire. This is the second death! Condemned to everlasting torment, they will have no rest, day or night, forever. So the axiom is very plain: born once,

die twice—born twice, die once. Which shall it be with you?
Have you been born again?

We have an imperative, that is true, but it contains within
itself the germ of a promise. For if it is true that we must be
born again, then it is also true that we may be born again.
There is a land of beginning again, a land where at the door
we can slough off our old lives like worn-out coats and enter
anew. We can be forgiven. We can be re-created. We can have
new hearts, new affections, new life, new power, new purpose, new direction, new destinations. Yes, we may be born
again. That, my friends, is *good news!*

Jesus, in the third chapter of John, describes to us the
mechanism whereby a man is born again. He says, "The wind
bloweth where it listeth, and thou hearest the sound thereof,
but canst not tell whence it cometh, and whither it goeth: so
is every one that is born of the Spirit" (v. 8). The Holy Spirit
is the agent of our regeneration. You will notice that the construction is passive as far as we are concerned. We do not
"born" ourselves. We "are born again." We are begotten by
God. We are created anew. We are new creatures. We are the
workmanship of God. We are the objects, and God is the subject. Regeneration is something God does to us with His
almighty power. The agent is the Holy Spirit, and the instru-
ment is the Word of God, the gospel of Jesus Christ.

Christ, in this very chapter, declares, "As Moses lifted up
the serpent in the wilderness [a sign of sin, and those who
looked at that serpent were healed of those fatal bites of
snakes that infested that area], even so must the Son of Man
be lifted up: that whosoever believeth in him should not perish, but have eternal life" (vv. 14–15). Christ has been lifted

up on the cross, and He has taken upon Himself our guilt; and so He is the serpent, the sign of evil, the most sin-laden, sin-cursed man that ever lived; and it is our sin that is imputed to Him, that is reckoned to Him. In our place, He stands there looking up into the frown of His Father, and God looks down upon His only Son in whom He is well pleased; and God pours out His wrath from sin upon His own Son. Jesus, in our place, descends into hell. Our sins will be punished upon us in hell or upon Christ on the cross; it depends on whether or not we trust in Him. There is life for a look at the crucified One. "Look unto me, and be ye saved, all the ends of the earth: for I am God, and there is none else" (Isaiah 45:22).

Have you been born again? If so, you are trusting in Jesus Christ and not in yourself. You have turned from your own righteousness. The great theologian Dr. John Gerstner of Pittsburgh said that so often the only thing that stands between God and sinners is the sinners' virtue. They have no righteousness in reality, but in them their righteousness is real, their virtues an illusion. Because they will not give up their trust in their own goodness and acknowledge their sin and trust in Christ, these form an impenetrable barrier between the sinners and the Savior. We have nothing to contribute to our salvation, my friends, except one thing: our sin. That is our total contribution. Our faith and our repentance are the work of God's grace in our hearts. Our contribution is simply the sin for which Jesus Christ suffered and died.

Would you be born anew? There has never been a person who sought for the new birth who did not find it. Even the seeking is created by the Spirit of God. Would you know that new life? Are you tired of the emptiness and purposelessness of your life? Are you tired of the filthy rags of your own righteousness? Would you trust in Someone other than yourself? Then look to the cross of Christ. Place your trust in Him. Ask Him to come in and be born in you today. For Jesus came into the world from glory to give us second birth because we must—we *must*—be born again.

CHAPTER THIRTEEN

WHY I BELIEVE IN THE HOLY SPIRIT

Know ye not that ye are the temple of God, and that the Spirit of God dwelleth in you?
1 CORINTHIANS 3:16

O f all the doctrines of the Christian faith, the one that causes the most trouble for many people seems to be that of the Holy Spirit. This is not surprising. In the introduction to this book, I said that my reason for writing it lay in the amazing number of Americans who are confused about who Jesus Christ is. I have found that even more people are confused about the fact that who He is—the carpenter of Galilee who is and was and ever shall be the eternal, omnipotent Creator and God Almighty of this universe—constitutes the cardinal doctrine of the Christian religion. How natural, then, that even less is understood about the Holy Spirit.

Presenting the biblical evidence for what I believe about the Holy Spirit is the most effective way I can think of for stating why I believe in the Holy Spirit. At the same time, finding out who the Bible says the Holy Spirit is, what He does, and how we may receive His blessings should clear away the confusion about Him.

Let's look at that first question: Who is the Holy Spirit? . . . Or should we say: What is the Holy Spirit? An "It"? Or "He"? Or, perchance, a "She"? The Holy Spirit has been called all three by men and women. One strange cult tried to create something like an earthly family with a father, a mother, and son by calling the Holy Spirit a "she." But the Bible never mentions anything like this.

On the other hand, many people refer to the Holy Spirit as "it"—a force, a thing, a power, an influence. But is that what the Holy Spirit is? Or is the Holy Spirit a person? The Bible makes it clear, I believe, that the Holy Spirit is a person. However, the use of the word *person* is not intended to conjure up an image of a stick figure with arms, legs, fingers, and toes. Rather, let us use the true sense of the word, in which *person* means "that which has personality, that is, will, intellect, emotion, ability to communicate," and so on.

In the Old Testament, the Holy Spirit is not clearly revealed, and the Jews very easily and understandably mistook the Spirit for being simply a power, an influence of God. The distinctions in the triune Godhead—the Father, Son, and Holy Spirit—though present, were also not clearly revealed to them. As Dr. Benjamin B. Warfield, professor of systematic theology at Princeton Theological Seminary, said, "The Old Testament is like a richly furnished but dimly lit room; in the New Testament nothing is added except light."

Of course, there are today those who deny the personality of the Holy Spirit on the basis that the Bible doesn't say in so many words that the Holy Spirit is a person. I acknowledge that it doesn't. But neither does the Bible set forth arguments to prove that God exists; this is something that is plainly revealed and understood. And so it is with the Holy Spirit.

But now let's look and see: What is a person? What is a thing? What is a force? We are told by some that the Holy Spirit is a force, like electricity or the wind or gravity. What is the difference between a force and a person? Let's take the matter of intellect: Does electricity have a mind? Does the wind have a mind? Does gravity have intellect? Of course not. Take the matter of emotion: Did you ever hear of electricity or gravity laughing? crying? loving? Consider communication: Can a force express its thoughts? No! Electricity may be used to run a machine that will repeat people's words, but it cannot communicate. Does it have a will to decide that it will do this? Is it self-motivated, or is it governed merely by external laws or by persons who direct it? *It* has no will of its own. A *person* does.

What do the Scriptures say about the Holy Spirit? Listen and judge for yourself. Is the Holy Spirit a force as the cultists say, or is He a person as the church of Christ says? The Bible refers to the mind of the Spirit: "He that searcheth the hearts knoweth what is the mind of the Spirit, because he maketh intercession for the saints" (Romans 8:27). The Holy Spirit has a mind; He makes intercession; He pleads for them. The Scriptures speak of the infinite comprehension of the Spirit: "The things of God knoweth no man, but the Spirit of God" (1 Corinthians 2:11). A force does not comprehend, but a person does. We have reference to the will of the Spirit: "Dividing to every man severally as he will" (1 Corinthians 12:11) is a reference to the Holy Spirit. Yet a force has no will.

The Holy Spirit not only knows but even foreknows: "He will declare to you the things that are to come" (John 16:13 RSV). Certainly wind, electricity, or any force knows neither what is now nor what is to come. The Bible refers to the love of the Spirit: "Now I beseech you . . . for the love of the Spirit" (Romans 15:30). We see that He acts; He strives: "My spirit shall not always strive with man" (Genesis 6:3). He commands and forbids: "The Holy Ghost said, Separate me Barnabas and Saul for the work whereunto I have called them" (Acts 13:2). He appoints officers in the church: ". . . the flock, over the which the Holy Ghost hath made you overseers" (Acts 20:28). He hears: "Whatsoever he shall hear, that shall he speak" (John 16:13). He speaks about many things: about events in latter times, about the Son of Man. He cries in the hearts of Christians, "Abba, Father" (Romans 8:15). "Yea, saith the Spirit, that they may rest from their labours; and their works do follow them" (Revelation 14:13). The Spirit said to Philip, "Go near, and join thyself to this chariot" (Acts 8:29). We see that all the attributes of personality are given to the Holy Spirit. The Holy Spirit is a person.

Some people nevertheless will disagree on the basis that, in the Greek, neuter pronouns are sometimes combined with the word for "spirit." But there is a very natural explanation for this. "Spirit" in Greek is *pneuma*, just like the Old Testament word meaning "breath," originally, and "wind." When the Holy Spirit is revealed, this is the name He takes.

Since *pneuma* is neuter gender in Greek, it is referred to by neuter pronouns. But rather than negating the fact of the personality of the Holy Spirit, this very grammatical rule serves to reinforce it, since there are instances in the New Testament where, contrary to expected usage, masculine pronouns are used to refer to the Holy Spirit.

To clarify our belief—our doctrine of the Holy Spirit—we must ascertain not only that He is a person but also that He is divine. Here again the Bible answers. In the Book of Acts we read that Peter said to Ananias, "Why hath Satan filled thine heart to lie to the Holy Ghost?" (5:3). When shortly thereafter Peter says to Ananias, "You have not lied to men but to God" (v. 4 RSV), he makes it evident that the Holy Spirit is God. The Scriptures expressly describe all the attributes of divinity and ascribe them to the Holy Spirit. "Whither shall I go from thy Spirit?" (Psalm 139:7). He is infinite, omnipresent: He knows all things; He knows the future; He is all-powerful.

I believe, however, that we must understand that the Holy Spirit is not merely another name for God the Father, but that there is a distinction of the personalities of the Godhead. This is clearly seen in a number of places. The baptismal formula requires us to be baptized in the name of the Father, and of the Son, and of the Holy Spirit—one name, three persons. In the baptism of Jesus, we see the Holy Spirit descend as a dove and the Father speak from above the clouds: "This is my beloved Son, in whom I am well pleased" (Matthew 3:17). The three personalities are thus clearly revealed. The same truth is affirmed again in the Bible in many places, including Christ's penetrating words in what we call the Great

Commission: "Go therefore and make disciples of all nations, baptizing them in the name of the Father and of the Son and of the Holy Spirit" (Matthew 28:19 RSV).

In spite of all the clear teachings of Scripture, however, one ancient heresy persists in some places even today. "Modalism," from the word *mode*, teaches that the Holy Spirit is a divine person but that He is simply the Father or the Son. This is like saying, in effect, that the Father first came out on stage as an actor with a long beard; then He went backstage, changed His costume, and returned to the stage as a young man, the Son; going backstage again, He then returned in yet another costume as the Spirit—just one person, in three disguises. But the Bible teaches that the Godhead is a triune Godhead of three personalities within the one substance of God, coeternal, existing side by side forever: "In the beginning was the Word, and the Word was with God" (John 1:1).

I believe in the Holy Spirit not only because of who the Bible says He is but also because of what the Bible says He does. The Scriptures give us an amazing report of His activities. Certainly, the list is far too long to include here, but among His works are such as these: He created the world, the world being created out of the Father through the Son and by the Holy Spirit. The Holy Spirit inspired the writing of the Scriptures so that the Bible is not like any other book, but God the Holy Spirit is the author thereof working through the instrumentality of men. The Holy Spirit caused Christ to be conceived in the womb of Mary, of whom it is said, "The Holy Ghost shall come upon thee." It was the Holy Spirit who baptized Jesus, who led Him and empowered Him. The Holy Spirit is also described as having raised

Jesus from the dead. The Holy Spirit, being poured out upon people, is the One who brought the Christian church into existence on Pentecost.

The Holy Spirit regenerates men and quickens them from their deadness in sin. Jesus said that we must be born again of the Spirit. Unless we have been regenerated by the Spirit, we are not Christians. The Holy Spirit indwells every Christian: "Know ye not that ye are the temple of God, and that the Spirit of God dwelleth in you?" (1 Corinthians 3:16). The Holy Spirit sanctifies, cleanses, makes pure and holy, and thus particularly is the Holy Spirit. The Holy Spirit does not come to glorify Himself or magnify Himself; you notice that He does not even have a distinctive name. Jesus said, "When the Comforter is come . . . he shall testify of me" (John 15:26).

When the Holy Spirit comes upon someone, one of the evidences is that the person speaks concerning the wonderful works God wrought in Christ the Redeemer. The Holy Spirit is the One who brings grace and enables the Christian to live the Christian life. "The fruit of the Spirit is love, joy, peace, longsuffering, gentleness, goodness, faith, meekness, temperance" (Galatians 5:22–23).

A further reason I believe in the Holy Spirit is the experience of His indwelling. Those who know the Spirit know that they have received "the earnest" of their inheritance, for the Holy Spirit also gives us the assurance that we have eternal life. It is the Holy Spirit who bears witness with our spirits that we are the children of God. It is the Holy Spirit who cries out, "Abba, Father," and makes us know that God is our Father and we are His sons and daughters who have been redeemed and are on our way to heaven. It is the Holy Spirit who can enable us as Christians to say, "Blessed assurance, Jesus is mine; O what a foretaste of glory divine." If we have that assurance and that certainty in our hearts, then we know that we have the Holy Spirit within us.

The Bible says that every believer receives the Holy Spirit when he or she becomes a Christian. But then we are to seek to be filled with the Holy Spirit, for we are leaky vessels. We need to have the fullness of His presence. I believe the reason there are so many defeated and downcast Christians is that they are not filled with the Holy Spirit. In our homes, is there love, joy, peace, longsuffering, gentleness? Or is there strife, discouragement, bickering, worry, anxiety, sadness? All these are evidences that the Spirit of God is not there, for He is the Spirit of joy and peace and love. The love of God is shed abroad in our hearts through the Holy Spirit.

If the fullness of the Spirit of God is missing in your life and you would like to know it, if you want to live and serve God as He would have you do, I have a suggestion for you to try. Dr. Bill Bright asked this of the people of our church at a service many years ago, and it had a profound effect at that time. He recommended to all those who wanted to be not merely hearers of the Word but doers also, that they go home, find a good-sized piece of paper, and on it write down all the specific sins present in their lives. List the sins of disposition, he said: impatience, bitterness, jealousy, envy, grudges held, slights unforgiven, animosity, anger, lust, lasciviousness, unclean thoughts, greed, cupidity, avarice, and so on. Be specific; name names, was the instruction. Don't forget the sins of omission: prayerlessness, cold-heartedness to God, faithlessness to His Word, service unrendered, witness not given, and other such sins—not hiding them in our hearts and failing to meditate on them.

Dr. Bright then instructed us to pray that the Holy Spirit would search and try us to see if there was still anything wicked in us that we had not confessed and forsaken. When the Holy Spirit brought something else to mind as we waited before Him, we wrote it down. We waited and asked again, "Holy Spirit of God, search me and try my heart, and see if there is still anything wicked in me." We continued to ask and wait, until we could genuinely come before God with a conscience free of offense toward Him and our fellow human beings. I can think of no greater blessing. Even this doesn't mean we are perfect, of course, but it means there is nothing that will come to mind that we will not confess, repent of, and forsake.

Now, write in large letters across the page (or pages): "The blood of Jesus Christ cleanses us from all sin." Claim that promise by faith. Believe it. At this point, for the first time, perhaps, you will be ready to do what Jesus said—to ask the Father to fill you with the Holy Spirit. "If ye then, being evil, know how to give good gifts unto your children: how much more shall your heavenly Father give the Holy Spirit to them that ask him?" (Luke 11:13). Ask the Father for the Holy Spirit. He cannot come when we are filled with self and with sin, with self-righteousness and pride and a pharisaical spirit. If we humble ourselves before God and confess our sins and our stiff-necked attitude, then God will come and fulfill His promise and fill us with His Spirit—the Spirit of love and the Spirit of joy. He will give us a new heart—a soft heart.

Now take the paper and burn it. (On one occasion when I asked a congregation to try this mode of confession, someone asked me, "What are we going to do, sign this and turn it in? That might land you in prison!") 'Tear it up! Throw it away! But claim the promise and believe God and go forth to live and walk in the Spirit and serve Him by the power of His Spirit. "Be filled with the Holy Spirit" (Acts 9:17 RSV).

Here is our challenge. James says, let's not be like those who hear the Word and go away and do nothing about it; or like those who behold their faces in a mirror and go away and forget how they look. I believe that it is only as we ask for this cleansing and fullness of the Holy Spirit that we will enter into an experience of blessedness, a closeness, and a realization of the presence of God in our lives that we have never known before.

CHAPTER FOURTEEN

WHY I BELIEVE
IN THE RETURN
OF CHRIST

Behold, he cometh with clouds, and every eye shall see him, and they also which pierced him: and all kindreds of the earth shall wait because of him. Even so, Amen.

REVELATION 1:7

The world has gone amuck! That is the conclusion of many of the deepest thinkers of the secular world of our time. Paul Johnson, one of the sophisticated statesmen in London, surveying the chaotic situation erupting around the world, concluded: "There are times when I feel that I would welcome an invasion from Mars."[1] A world gone out of control. I can assure you that there will be an invasion, but it will not come from Mars. It will come from farther away than that, for it will be the invasion of the Son of God, the Creator returning to His creation. Jesus Christ will come again!

Our subject is exceedingly relevant in these climactic times. Why do I believe in the return of Christ? First and foremost, for the simple reason that Jesus Christ Himself declares it to be so. He said, "Let not your heart be troubled: ye believe in God, believe also in me. In my Father's house are many mansions: if it were not so, I would have told you. I go to prepare a place for you. And if I go and prepare a place for you, I will come again, and receive you unto myself; that where I am, there ye may be also" (John 14:1–3). Jesus Christ is coming again.

For almost two thousand years the church has been declaring in its creeds that Jesus Christ shall come to judge the quick and the dead. There have been some quacks who have given the whole doctrine a bad name by majoring in this entirely; however, we must not let that cause us to lose sight of the fact that the entire historic Christian church had believed emphatically that Jesus Christ would return to this world. This belief is found in the Apostles' Creed, the Nicene Creed, the Constantinopolitan Creed, and in all the ancient ecumenical creeds of the church. It is found in the Westminster Confession of Faith, which contains the doctrinal standards of the whole Presbyterian world. It is found in the Thirty-nine Articles of the Church of England, the Anglican standards, and it is found in the Augsburg Confession of the Lutherans. Throughout Christendom, we find unanimous consent that Jesus Christ *will* return to this world!

There have been scoffers who have said, "Where is the promise of his coming? for since the fathers fell asleep, all things continue as they were from the beginning of the creation" (2 Peter 3:4). The scoffers are willfully ignorant of this fact. God is not slack concerning His promise, but He desires that men would repent, turn from their sins, and be saved. He has patiently waited for almost two thousand years. The Scripture declares it, the Old Testament proclaims it, the apostles affirmed it. This fact is declared more than three hundred times throughout the Old and New Testaments: Jesus Christ will come again. The apostle John said, "Every eye shall see him, and they also which pierced him: and all kindreds of the earth shall wail because of him. . . . Even so, come, Lord Jesus" (Revelation 1:7; 22:20).

Do you really want to know if you are a Christian? Ask yourself if you can honestly make this statement, "Even so, come, Lord Jesus." If we do not belong to Him, then we cannot say that because His coming will fill with an unnamed foreboding those who do not know that they belong to Him.

I further believe that Jesus Christ will return because the entire Christian view of history demands it. The ancient Greeks believed that history was cycling, going round and round like an eternal merry-go-round. For the Christian, however, the biblical view of history is linear. It is moving ever onward, inexorably, toward a great climactic conclusion—the consummation of the ages—when God will drop the final curtain upon the drama of this world. Jesus Christ, who once came in humility, will come back again in glory—a glory that will eclipse the sun, with ten thousand times ten thousand of His saints. He will come with the angels of heaven, with the sound of a trumpet, and He will take unto Himself His own, who shall be caught up to be with the Lord forever. Those who have ignored Him, denied Him, pretended but never really repented of their sins, shall be consumed with everlasting destruction—in flaming fire.

Lord Shaftesbury, who did more perhaps for the social reform of England than any other person, said: "I do not think that in the last forty years I have lived one conscious hour that was not influenced by the thought of our Lord's return. Having this hope, we purify ourselves. For justice also demands it." It is sadly true that so often the righteous have been oppressed and have been persecuted. Even now, more than a million Christians languish in Siberian prison camps inside Russia alone. Too often the wicked prosper, yet Scripture says not to envy them but to consider their end, for their final end will be one of destruction. Justice demands that Christ return in judgment. A culmination of all the purposes of God and the kingdom of God shall be reached. I believe this is the only hope for a world that has gone awry.

I also believe in Christ's return because of the signs that Scripture declares will precede it. I am not a prophet and neither do I have much confidence in those who endeavor to establish specific dates regarding the return of Christ; the Scripture clearly states that we know not the day or the hour.

Christina Rossetti was watching a great symphony orchestra and she noticed that suddenly, in a twinkling of an eye, at a precise moment, every hand reached out and turned the page of music. Her thoughts flitted to the Scripture, and she realized that it would be just that way—suddenly in a moment every eye would look up and every head would turn to see the Lord coming in indescribable glory.

The Bible declares there are signs of those things that will precede His coming. Those signs have existed in some degree down through the centuries; however, they exist in thunderous fashion today. Great cumulative evidence seems to point ineluctably toward the fact that soon—soon—Christ will come. Billy Graham visited the heads of every state in the Free World and found that only one believed there was any hope for this world beyond the end of this century.

Christ will come!

What are some of those signs?

The Scripture says that there will be earthquakes. There have always been earthquakes, so what is the significance of that? Evidently it means that there will be earthquakes in a unique way—in number and severity. One of the great historians of seismology, Don Leet, after nearly a lifetime of study, said: "In the fourteenth century, there were 137 earthquakes; in the fifteenth century, 174; in the sixteenth century, 253; in 1971 and similarly since there have been 18,000 earthquakes in the world!"[2]

We are told that men's hearts will fail them for fear. Bertrand Russell, the unbelieving British philosopher who wrote the book *Why I Am Not a Christian*, said: "The best we can hope for is unyielding despair." Jean Paul Sartre, the French existentialist, said the very same thing, "Unyielding despair, and upon this foundation we must build our lives."

Dr. John Wesley White, a Ph.D. from Oxford, points out a number of different evidences for the fact that Christ's return is apparently near. On CBS television an interview was conducted with avant-garde playwrights Susan Sontag and Agnes Varda. It was pointed out that in recent times most of the films for the youth culture have had one prevailing theme—doom and despair. Sixteen- and seventeen-year-olds were even more pessimistic than college students.³ In America and Canada today the number one cause of death of college students is suicide. A nation of despair! Many older people do not understand that, because they have not been exposed to the type of thoughts that these young people are continually bombarded with in the universities. Young people are looking for a place to hide, a cop-out, somewhere to flee. They have fled into the drug culture, the communes, and the mystic religions of Asia trying to find a place to hide. One youth song is titled "No Hiding Place."

We are told there will be a great explosion of learning in the last times, people will be ever learning and yet never able to come to the truth. In twenty-four hours we now learn more than was learned in two thousand years of antiquity. An explosion of knowledge! Sadly, many seem unable to grasp the knowledge of the ultimate truth—of Him who is truth itself. This great quest for knowledge was seen as the panacea and the savior of mankind. The humanist redeemer—education—was going to redeem the world from poverty, crime, and delinquency.

Has it become this panacea? The government spent millions of dollars on a study to determine how effectively education diminished crime. Surprisingly, all the statistics studied demonstrated incontestably that education elevates crime: the more education, the more crime. The same conclusion was reached by sociologist Dr. Ray Jeffrey, who has demonstrated beyond all doubt that education, if not accompanied by some moral or spiritual elevator, escalates crime.⁴

What is needed is some moral revolution, some spiritual endowment to change the heart of man. The monsters of the

Nazi atrocities were for the most part extraordinarily educated men. At the time the Nazi scourge broke upon the earth, Nazi Germany was the best-educated country in the world. No, education is not the humanist redeemer that men thought it would be. These conclusions have led many of the enlightened and intelligent people of our day to a great fear, as the Scripture says that men's hearts will be failing them for fear in the last days.

Professor Harold Ure, a Nobel prize winner and a leading scientist and evolutionist of our time, said in his book *Man Afraid*, "I write this to frighten you. I am a frightened man myself. All the scientists I know are frightened—frightened for their lives and frightened for your life."[5] Men's hearts are failing them for fear. The number one cause of death in the world today is heart failure, just as the Scripture said that it would be. If we knew what is going on in the experimental laboratories, we, too, would be frightened. It is only our blissful ignorance that keeps us from the same fear Professor Urey described. Bertrand Russell, looking back over the years of his life, wrote, "I could think of nothing but suicide. . . . Over man and all his works, night falls pitiless and dark."[6]

A world of despair. Scientists tell us that they have a hydrogen bomb that can be encased in cobalt and that, if exploded over the North Pole, would kill every living creature in the whole Northern Hemisphere of this planet. Three billion people! The doomsday machine.

We are also told that there will be pestilence. We have seen a breakout of the black death, unheard of since the Middle Ages; the bubonic plague has taken thousands of lives in Pakistan. Other diseases, not seen in centuries, are reappearing, and new ones, such as the AIDS virus, are appearing and wreaking incredible havoc. Venereal diseases are producing strains totally resistant to all known antibiotics. It has been reported that we have developed bacteriological weapons so awesome that if the public knew about them, production would probably be banned. There is one such weapon that if released into the atmosphere would kill every human being on this planet. Hundreds of thousands of people have died in famines in Biafra, Pakistan, India, and Cambodia. This is just a prelude to the mass famine that is anticipated—famine that could precipitate wars on a large and global scale never before seen.

In spite of the fact that we live in the so-called age of peace, since World War II, Dr. John Wesley White tells us, there have been two thousand books written on the subject of peace.[7] In fact, we have less peace now than we have ever had. A Jewish rabbi, Joshua Liebman, wrote *Peace of Mind;* a Catholic bishop, Fulton J. Sheen, *Peace of Soul;* and Billy Graham, *Peace with God.* Yet, on all sides, we hear of wars and rumors of wars. The Soviet Union has crumbled. One would think that would make the world safer and freer, but its suddenly free Baltic countries fell into horrifying civil wars, and madmen in the Middle East are stockpiling banned weapons, including nuclear ones, that have the rest of the world so worried that the United States, now the only superpower left, has had to repeatedly use our nation's armed forces' power against these small nation dictators to safeguard the entire world.

The Scripture tells us that in the days of Noah there was unlicensed sexual behavior. Certainly we are seeing that in our time. It is worth remembering that God's destruction of great parts of mankind has always been connected with sexual immorality. This was true in the time of Noah before God destroyed almost all in the Flood. It was true in the time of Sodom when God rained fire and brimstone upon the cities of the plain, and they disappeared beneath the south end of the Dead Sea. It was also true of the Canaanites whom God destroyed because of their sexual immorality, and particularly because of their perversion, causing the land to vomit them. What must God be thinking about America today?

When Jesus Christ comes, He will come as Savior of His own and Judge of the rest. For those who do not trust Him, for those who do not love Him and who are not His own, it will be a time of great fear. Men shall cry out for the hills to cover them and for the mountains to fall upon them and hide them from the face of Him that sitteth upon the throne. From that incongruous phrase "the wrath of the Lamb" (Revelation 6:16) When a lamb becomes wrathful, that is a day to fear. Are we ready? What if it were today?

Tragically, there are millions in the church who have been satisfied to substitute churchianity for Christianity. They have been satisfied with the externalities and never had the reality of Christ within their hearts. They have never repented of their sins and surrendered to Christ as Lord and Master of their lives. They know they are still sitting on the throne of their lives—they do what they want to do when they want to do it. They have never yielded themselves in complete surrender to Christ. They have never put their trust in Him. They have never received the gift of eternal life. Consequently, there is one inescapable fact. Deep in their hearts they do not know that they have eternal life. Yet the Scripture says that we can. We must.

If we have trusted in Jesus Christ and invited Him to come in and take over our lives, then we *know* that we have been forgiven. We *know* that we are on our way to heaven. We know that when He comes, He will take us to be with Him forever in glory—to that place He has prepared for us.

NOTES

Chapter 1

1. *National Enquirer,* 7 January 1975, 24, 25.
2. Charles Mercer, *Alexander the Great* (New York: Harper & Row, 1962), 61.

Chapter 2

1. R. A. Torrey, *The Higher Criticism and the New Theology* (Montrose: Montrose Christian Literature Society, 1911), 129.
2. Ibid., 134.
3. Ibid., 132.
4. Ibid., 130, 132, 133, 134.
5. Ibid., 140, 141.
6. William F. Albright, *The Archaeology of Palestine* (New York: Pelican Books, Penguin Books), 225.
7. Josh McDowell, *Evidence That Demands a Verdict* (San Bernardino, Calif.: Campus Crusade for Christ, 1972), 71.
8. William F. Albright, *The Biblical Period from Abraham to Ezra* (New York: Harper & Row, 1960).
9. McDowell, *Evidence*, 70.
10. Ibid., 72.
11. T. W. Fawthrop, *The Stones Cry Out* (London: Marshall, Morgan & Scott, Ltd., 1934), 46.
12. Ibid.
13. McDowell, *Evidence*, 68.
14. Ibid.

Chapter 3

1. Mortimer Adler and William Gorman, eds., *The Great Ideas, A*

Syntopicon of Great Books of the Western World (Chicago: Encyclopaedia Britannica, 1952), 53.

2. James Reid, *God, the Atom, and the Universe* (Grand Rapids, Mich.: Zondervan Publishing House, 1968), 1.

3. Ibid., chap. 1.

4. E. L. Woodward, *Is It—Or Isn't It?*

5. Pierre Simon de La Place, *Evidences of Revelation,* 7.

6. Quoted in Fred John Meldan, *Why We Believe in Creation Not in Evolution* (Denver: Christian Victory Publishing Co., 1959), 27.

7. William Paley, *Natural Theology* (New York: American Tract Society, n.d.), 30–31.

8. Meldan, *Why We Believe in Creation,* 225.

9. Ibid., 238.

10. Henry M. Morris, *The Bible Has the Answer* (Grand Rapids: Baker Book House, 1971), 16.

11. *American Magazine,* November 1930.

Chapter 4

1. Louis T. More, *The Dogma of Evolution* (Princeton: University Press, 1925), 160.

2. Quoted in Henry M. Morris, *Scientific Creationism* (San Diego: Creation-Life Publishers, 1974), 8.

3. Quoted in Meldan, *Why We Believe in Creation,* 8.

4. Quoted in James F. Coppedge, *Evolution: Possible or Impossible?* (Grand Rapids: Zondervan Publishing House, 1973), 180.

5. Robert T. Clark and James D. Bales, *Why Scientists Accept Evolution* (Grand Rapids: Baker Book House, 1966).

6. Henry M. Morris, *The Troubled Waters of Evolution* (San Diego: Creation-Life Publishers, 1974), 58.

7. Quoted in H. Enoch, *Evolution or Creation?* (London: Evangelical Press, 1966), v.

8. Quoted in Coppedge, *Evolution,* 177.

9. *Time,* 30 December 1974, 48.

10. Ibid.

11. Coppedge, *Evolution,* chap 6.

12. Ibid., 166–67.

13. Quoted in Enoch, *Evolution or Creation?*, 22.

14. Quoted in *Did Man Get Here by Evolution or Creation?* (New York: Watchtower Bible Tract, 1967), 45.

15. Quoted in Morris, *Troubled Waters,* 91.

16. Quoted in Duane Gish, *Evolution—The Fossils Say No!* (San Diego: Creation-Life Publishers, 1978), 14.

17. Quoted in Enoch, *Evolution or Creation?*, 67.

18. Ibid., 28.

Chapter 5

1. Leslie D. Weatherhead, *After Death* (New York: Abingdon Press, 1936), 19.

2. Thomas Curtis Clark, ed., *The Golden Book of Immortality* (New York: Association Press, 1954), 4.

3. Madison C. Peters, *After Death—What?* (New York: Christian Herald, 1908), 165.

4. Quoted in Weatherhead, *After Death,* 22.

5. Quoted in Peters, *After Death—What?,* 25.

6. Watson Boone Duncan, *Immortality and Modern Thought* (Boston: Sherman, French & Co., 1912), 33, 36.

7. Alfred Lord Tennyson, "Crossing the Bar," ll. 13–16.

8. "Heaven and Earth," ll. 111–14.

9. Joseph Addison, *Cato, A Tragedy* (New York: Effingham Maynard & Co., 1891), act 5, sc. 1, ll. 1861–67.

10. Quoted in Peters, *After Death—What?,* 166–67.

11. S. B. Shaw, *How Men Face Death* (Kansas City: Beacon Hill Press, 1964), 44, 63.

12. Raymond A. Moody, Jr., *Life After Life* (Atlanta: Mockingbird Books, 1975), 37.

Chapter 6

1. A. A. Hodge, *Popular Lectures on Theological Themes* (Philadelphia: Presbyterian Board of Publications, 1887), 456–57.

2. Joseph C. Stiles, *Future Punishment* (St. Louis: n.p.,1868), 4.

3. Hodge, *Popular Lectures,* 454.

4. William Edward Munsey, *Eternal Retribution* (Murfreesboro, Tenn.: Sword of the Lord Publishers, 1951), 65.

5. Ibid., 62.

6. Ibid., 63.

7. Ibid.

Chapter 7

1. Carl F. H. Henry, *Christian Personal Ethics* (Grand Rapids, Mich: Wm. B. Eerdmans, 1957), 13.

Chapter 8

1. Philip Schaff, *The Person of Christ* (Boston: The American Tract Society, 1865), 6.

2. Ibid.

3. J. Gilchrist Lawson, *Greatest Thoughts About Jesus Christ* (New York: Richard R. Smith, Inc., 1919), 160.

4. Schaff, *The Person of Christ,* 5.

5. *The Ante-Nicene Fathers,* vol. 8 (Grand Rapids, Mich: Wm. B. Eerdmans, 1951), 460, 461.

6. Quoted in McDowell, *Evidence,* 86.

7. Ibid., 83.

8. Ibid., 84.

9. Ibid., 85, 86.

10. Ibid., 87.

11. Philip Schaff, *Testimonies of Unbelievers* (Boston: The American Tract Society, 1865), 281.

12. Quoted in McDowell, *Evidence,* 84, 85.

13. Quoted in Schaff, *The Person of Christ,* 108.

14. Ibid., 295–96.

15. Ibid., 316–17.

16. Quoted in Lawson, *Greatest Thoughts,* 117–20.

17. Ibid., 120–21.

18. Ibid., 147.

Chapter 10

1. Simon Greenleaf, *The Testimony of the Evangelists* (1874; reprint ed., Grand Rapids, Mich: Baker Book House, 1965), 28–30.

2. Paul Little, *Know Why You Believe* (Wheaton, Ill.: Victor Books, 1967), 44.

3. Quoted in William M. Taylor, *The Miracle of Our Saviour* (New York: Hodder & Stoughton, 1890), 21, 22.

4. Frank Morison, *Who Moved the Stone?* (1930; reprinted Whitstable: Latimer Trend & Co., 1971), 114–15.

5. Quoted in Wilbur M. Smith, *Therefore, Stand* (Grand Rapids: Baker Book House, 1945), 383.

6. Ibid., 378.

Chapter 11

1. Quoted in Earle Albert Rowell, *Prophecy Specks* (Washington, D.C.: Review and Herald Publishing Co., 1938), 67.

Chapter 12

1. Quoted in James Hastings, *The Great Texts of the Bible,* vol. 2 (Grand Rapids: Wm. B. Eerdmans), 149.

2. Walter Russell Bowie, *Men of Fire* (New York: Harper Bros., 1961), chap. 6.

Chapter 14

1. Quoted in John Wesley White, *Re-entry* (Minneapolis: World Wide Publications, 1970), 106.

2. Ibid., 54.

3. John Wesley White, *WW III: Signs of the Impending Battle of Armageddon* (Grand Rapids: Zondervan Publishing House, 1977), 82.

4. Quoted in White, *Re-entry,* 93.

5. Ibid., 104.

6. Ibid., 100.

7. Ibid., 96.

8. Ibid., 97.